LEAD CHANGE WITHOUT FEAR

Using The YES I AM Solution

PAUL SCHNITZLER PH. D.

Copyright © 2015 by Paul Schnitzler Ph. D.
All rights reserved. This book or any portion thereof may not be reproduced or used in any manner whatsoever without the express written permission of the publisher except for the use of brief quotations in a book review.

Printed in the United States of America
First Printing, 2015

Wesley Chapel, Florida
www.leadchangewithoutfear.com

ISBN: 1500743674
ISBN 13: 9781500743673
Library of Congress Control Number: 2014914090
CreateSpace Independent Publishing Platform
North Charleston, South Carolina

DEDICATION

This book is dedicated to my father and mother, Jack and Mildred Schnitzler, and to my aunt Anne Spero who, together, civilized me. Sadly, none will see this book.

ACKNOWLEDGEMENTS

I give thanks every day for my wife, Sandra Miniere, who supported me in difficult times during the writing of this book. She also has been a wealth of information about the process of writing and publishing. And she has been my most productively critical editor!

For digging in and spotting a number of last-minute oversights, I gratefully thank my daughter Robin Schnitzler Nathan.

Terry Don, was my first editor, and the first person to read the rough manuscript. Besides correcting the usual grammar, punctuation and word issues, she suggested some important structural changes and provided a sounding board for my ideas. Thank you, Terry.

I thank Tim Bolen who was my principal editor. He provided many valuable ideas including the suggestion to add the opening story. Tim has become a friend as well.

My long-time friend, Dr. Leonard Blank, suggested the notion of the overly confident leader which became the second problematic change I considered but more importantly opened my eyes to still others. Thank you, Len.

My students had little choice but to endure my teaching efforts. As you will see, my writing reflects my teaching style. I thank them for their feedback which I believe helped make this book effective.

I am grateful to Dr. Jose Zayas-Castro, Dr. Paul McCright, and Prof. Dolores Gooding for bringing me into USF and giving me the opportunity to teach Management of Technological Change. This started me on the path which led to this book. Paul was also the first non-editor to read the early manuscript, and he made valuable suggestions about content and book design; thank you Paul.

The manager does things right, the leader does the right thing.

Warren Bennis, 1989 [1]

TABLE OF CONTENTS

Dedication	iii
Acknowledgements	v
Prologue & Preface	1
The change that challenged me to lead…	1
Why I wrote this book	5
Chapter One—Introduction	7
Approaches to Change	10
My Approach and Solution	12
Chapter Two—Getting Started—The YES I AM Solution	19
Your Passion	22
Everyone benefits	26
Seek Their Ideas	31
Include Everyone	37
Ask for Help	42
Manage Uncertainty	48
Chapter Three—The Role of Control	53
Chapter Four—Taking Steps Toward the Goal	63
Form a Supportive Committee	64
Create Your Vision	66
Use Strong Communication Tools	68
Segment the Project	71
Chapter Five—Institutionalizing the Change	75
Relate to the Vision and Continue to Build	76
Integrate into the Organization's Culture	78

TABLE OF CONTENTS

Chapter Six—Change Examples: From Good to Awful	**81**
Successful Changes	82
Change So-So's	89
Failures	93
Chapter Seven—Change Failed? Not Yours!	**97**
The Anxious Leader	99
The Confident Leader	103
The Hurried Leader	107
The "Educated" Leader	110
The Mistrustful Leader	113
The Uninformed Leader	116
The Wrong-Change Leader	120
Epilogue & Summary	**123**
The change that challenged me to lead… (cont.)	123
The basic model revisited	126
List of Appendices	**129**
Appendix A Expanded Table of Contents	131
Appendix B What Kind of Change Leader Are You?	135
Appendix C Types of change and how they appear	139
Appendix D Short history of change	141
Bibliography	**143**

PROLOGUE & PREFACE

THE CHANGE THAT CHALLENGED ME TO LEAD...

Seated in my office during the summer of '78, I was puzzling over the design for our advanced undersea telephone communications system. Phil, my department head, burst in looking very excited. He rested a hip on the corner of my desk and asked me if I was familiar with fiber-optic laser communications systems. Of course I knew about them, but not very much. Up till then, virtually all long-distance communications used "analog" technology—solidly understood, and very dependable. I was aware that a few land-based installations used the new fiber-optic technology.

"Well," he said, "the company management decided that the next undersea system should use optical fiber technology."

I said, "That's exciting. What does that have to do with us? We know nothing about fiber design."

"True—but neither does anyone else in the company. And your group understands the peculiar needs of undersea systems.

"We would like your group to build a prototype to demonstrate feasibility."

Wow! At that time, optical fiber technology looked like the future for many uses. With this project, my engineers and I had the opportunity to get into this new area. "I'm listening."

"You can build on the technology that is in use in the land-based installations. The groups that designed those systems are available to help."

Sounded very good—so far.

"We want your target performance to be *six times* that of the land-based system."

'Wait a minute" I began.

"And you can have six months to complete the project!" he continued.

This seemed huge! "Let me get this straight. I am to lead the design of a system which will have six times the capacity of any commercial system. It must meet undersea rigors such as extreme pressure, and have a 25-year lifetime. We have six months to do this with a team of engineers who have never worked with digital systems, lasers or fiber optics. Right?"

"Right!" he said.

But can we do it, I wonder? Do I want to take the risk? "What else can you tell me?" I asked him cautiously.

"There is a group in the semiconductor division which is ready to help develop any special devices needed. Also, you can call on engineers in two of my other groups to be part of the project."

These groups had many fine engineers. The semiconductor division was also very strong. I knew many people in all of these areas.

How could I say no to this challenge?

The next day

My immediate group had about ten top-flight engineers; they were all men—remember this was 1978; women engineers were few and far between. I phoned each of my engineers to ask them to attend a meeting to discuss a new opportunity. (No emails in those days!) I also invited the two peer groups Phil told me I could involve.

We met that afternoon.

Skill sets: Analog vs. fiber/laser

I jumped right in and described the challenge that I had accepted.

There were questions and objections: "We are analog designers; how can we possibly to do this?" "What about the current advanced analog system? What will happen to it?" "Six months? Are you kidding?" "Lasers can never have the reliability that we will require!" "What were you thinking to accept this project?"

"Yes, it will not be easy but you are the best. I am certain you can learn what you need to know and solve problems as they arise. The current advanced analog system you are developing is truly exceptional; you know that. If you could do that, then I am certain that if an optical fiber system can be built, you guys can do it. Yes this will be a huge change in what you do and the skills you need. *And* it will give you a great start in this new field."

About now, I was starting to realize: *I don't know* what we actually must do! What are the elements of this hypothetical optical fiber system? Which engineer can I ask to do…what?

Oh boy! Now what do I do?

Participative management

I had recently taken a management development training session which focused on group process. Participative management (PM) was a key element in the program. At the time the notion appealed intellectually but how well would it work? I didn't know. The management trainers told us to let the members of the team participate equally in deciding what is to be done—and by whom. I wasn't so sure this would work Now, with this optical fiber system project I was starting to think I might have to try this participation thing.

First I needed to sort out what I needed to know: What, exactly, are the tasks that must be done? Who is to do each task? How do we decide how much time each task will take? Do we have a prayer of completing this in six months?

I decided that I *would* use PM— As Yoda said, "Try not! Do or do not. There is no try." So I decided to stick with it. There would not be time for a "Plan B." In fact, I realized, there *was* no other choice!

At our next meeting, I asked the group to help define the needed tasks. We listed them on "flip-chart" paper and stuck them on the walls.

Ideas came fast and even though no one had worked in this area, the ideas were very good.

We agreed to meet twice a week, and at each meeting we worked on refining the lists. Some items were changed, some deleted and new ones added.

Things were progressing.

Fear and anxiety—mine

But as two, then three weeks passed, I began to worry. The changes we made at each meeting were becoming smaller. And I didn't see how to get people assigned to the tasks.

I would ask the group "How can we decide who will do what?" but I couldn't get them to move on this.

What was I going to do? It was keeping me up at night!

At this critical point I felt stuck and worried. Little did I know that I was about to discover the principles that would eventually become the key ideas in the *YES I AM Solution* for success.

WHY I WROTE THIS BOOK

> Change initiatives usually fail. That's right, 70 percent of the time the desired results and benefits are not achieved! That need not be and that is why this book has been written. [2]

I worked in industry for most of my career. During that time I created products, started and ran businesses, and all the while I was creating change. These changes included introducing wholly new technologies, building businesses, improving processes, and more. It was great fun!

It never occurred to me that there was any difficulty introducing something new. If the change was correct, it simply worked.

When I started teaching a course called Management of Technological Change,* I naturally began reading about the subject. I found that there were well understood techniques to gain the desired outcomes. The writers all described the techniques I had been using.

So it was a surprise when I discovered that research reported that change initiatives usually fail.

Change initiatives fail in spite of the wisdom and proven methods from leading change management experts. This does not have to be. I wrote this book to encourage leaders to discover how their perceptions and behaviors may be sabotaging their plans and limiting their results. The ***YES I AM*** six-step model provides a foundation for leaders to launch successful change initiatives.

The experts said that when you follow their steps, successful change will follow. If these known tools work, why does change fail so often?

In this book, I will tell you
- Seven situations when change is likely to fail;
- Why failures occur;
- What you can do to succeed!

---
* College of Engineering, University of South Florida

While the examples I use are primarily from industry, the concepts and tools apply to change initiatives in most organizations—education, law, medicine, finance, fund-raising, retail and more. In fact, this book will apply to any change that involves more than one person—including personal or family matters!

Chapter One

INTRODUCTION

Change is a part of life; change initiatives are a necessary part of business

To help today's leaders introduce a change, diverse sources of knowledge are available: books galore (a search on Amazon for "change management" yields tens of thousands of hits), MBA programs (170,000 new MBAs each year [31]), workshops, online seminars and more. Realizing that leaders need help, organizational experts have provided it. Yet only 30 percent of change initiatives succeed.

Why is this so?

The first answer to this question must be that few leaders use this wealth of knowledge.

Why don't they use it?

Below are seven types of leaders who are failing because they are not doing the things that will make them successful:

1. Leaders who are anxious about the success of the change they are introducing.
2. Leaders who are completely confident of the technology and issues involved.
3. Leaders who decide that the change is so urgent that there is not enough time to use these tools.
4. Leaders who can tell you exactly what must be done in the change process but do not know how to do it.
5. Leaders who don't believe in the change process or in their employees.
6. Leaders who have no knowledge of change processes.
7. Leaders who simply introduce the wrong changes or don't even realize they are dealing with change!

INTRODUCTION

While the situations appear different, the negative behaviors are the same, and the solutions are also largely the same. In *Chapter 7—Change Failed? Not Yours!*, these seven leaders will be described in detail, and I will provide tools to help each one.

Appendix B has a short assessment "*What Kind of Change Leader Are You?*" It will help identify your leadership style.

How change is introduced

When an organization decides that things need to improve, what happens? The leader analyzes the situation, decides what is needed, and begins the process. The focus is on the change and the work is on the details that are necessary to achieve the results wanted. This might be done by the leader alone, with colleagues, or with an outside consultant who was brought in for advice.

Sometimes management announces coming changes with assurances that these changes will provide an important set of improvements. More often, though, *nothing* is said even after the change activities begin. In any case, the employees eventually find out—the rumor mill is very effective and often inaccurate—and they begin to wonder what is really happening. Naturally, they are concerned about how it will affect them.

Appendix C is a short description of "*Types of changes and how they appear.*"

The effect of change on employees

When employees start to think about what will happen to them, they may become anxious, and even fearful. They will spend time talking about the situation, worrying about their future, and generally becoming less productive.

In the workplace, an employee begins to think about all of the potential problems: Will I be able to do the new work? Will I like the new tasks? Will it take more time? I'm already spending too much time at work. Is my job at risk? Will I become unnecessary to the company?

If I, as an employee, don't know much about what will happen—suppose the boss has told us very little—I will try to learn more from my associates. We'll talk over coffee; we'll pass on rumors; we'll imagine what may happen; and we'll share horror stories from other companies, friends, and acquaintances.

All of this non-productive activity results in less being done for the company and diminishes the help available for the change to succeed.

The leader needs help from the employees to make the process succeed; instead, not only are the employees not helpful, they are often counterproductive. In addition, absenteeism and turnover will go up and, even when employees are present, their minds are elsewhere.

The leader's role and difficulties

For change to succeed, it is essential that the employees and everyone else affected want to do what is needed. This means that all of these people have to be engaged and empowered so that they will do their best to get the desired results.

It is the leader's role to make this happen. It can be a heavy burden and a major source of stress.

Leaders may feel concerned, anxious, and perhaps even fearful. In such cases, it is common to try to control everything and everyone. The leader will make certain that everyone knows what they are to do and then make certain these activities get done well.

Maintaining such control will prevent engaging and empowering the employees. Thus the leader has a conundrum: maintain control for peace of mind or take risks and empower employees to get the job done.

Appendix D provides a *"Short History of Change."*

INTRODUCTION

APPROACHES TO CHANGE

Now let's look at what these experts, books and schools teach.

Leaders need to help employees become more comfortable with what is happening. Teachers (in classes or in books) provide an array of tools which will help engage the employees and empower them to contribute to the success of the process, the success of the change.

These experts point out that by empowering your employees you show them that they are important and valued. That makes them want to help. Consequently, they dig in and work to make the project a success.

Motivating others often requires leaders to act against their strong inclinations: They must boldly do things which may feel unsafe, useless, or excessively time consuming. The unwillingness to take these actions is the reason for the high failure rate.

Leaders usually focus on the details of the change but it is the people who are going to be affected who hold the key to your project's success. They are your team members, employees, colleagues, and other stakeholders. Pass them by, and you may bypass your benefits.

However, there is one more person in the equation: You! The Leader is crucial to success, and few authors speak about this person's issues. **Lead Change without Fear** is all about the leader's contribution to success!

Success requires subordinates—and sometimes peers and even supervisors—to do more than simply cooperate. Yet these key people are often preoccupied with how the changes will affect them—negatively! They tend to worry that they will not be able to learn the new skills; or perhaps they will not like the new work. Their greatest concern: that their very jobs may be at risk. With these thoughts in their minds, their focus will not be on making your program work. They will not be focusing on getting the benefits. Their focus will be on the negative effects for themselves!

Experts have provided many ways to get the cooperation of these people: Help them see why the changes are vital to the company. Provide a Vision of how the new, improved company will look. Communicate this Vision over and over again. Empower them. Remove roadblocks—and more.

Empowerment is an important thread running through many of these tools: To use these tools, the Leader must give power or control to the employees. This is called "empowerment." Its very name conveys the idea of yielding control. If I give you power, I must be giving up some of my power. This is the reason why many leaders do not empower their employees: They are unwilling to give up power or control.

But don't miss this stunning paradox: As the leader, when I give others power, I actually have more power! My leadership has made them more effective; I get more credit and am given greater responsibility. This can be surprising.

Giving up power can be difficult for some people. Later we will see what conditions exacerbate this difficulty. And you will see why leaders frequently don't use these tools.

Once you are convinced that this approach will work, this book will provide specific tools to help you make it easier to empower your employees—and be comfortable at the same time.

In many of these cases, leaders may think they have all the facts. They are sure they can handle the situation themselves. However, employees may have some important knowledge which could help improve the whole change process. Leaders, in their certainty, fail to see what's missing, and this oversight can lead directly to failure. In the extreme, leaders may even be introducing the wrong change! All of these situations contain risks.

INTRODUCTION

MY APPROACH AND SOLUTION

What can be done to improve the odds for success? The answer to this question is the thesis of this book. I have not found the solution elsewhere so I created my own.* These are the issues I address:

- The Why of the failures
- The What of success
- The How to Do the What! (This may seem strange but often people "know" what to do but cannot actually act on that knowledge.)
- The Way to stay sane as you go through the process.
- The Convincers: Examples of successful, not so good, and failed change initiatives.
- The Places to go for help for the different types of leaders.

The *YES I AM Solution* is a model that helps the seven types of failure-prone leaders to develop productive behaviors. It provides explicit, useful methods to avoid these pitfalls. These methods are explained and taught through examples, exercises, and challenges. Through these activities, you will develop greater leadership skills and, in the process, will learn concrete ways to successfully achieve the results you want.

The core idea of the experts' teachings is that employees must want to help. The experts tell leaders to empower their employees, include them in the change process, keep them informed, and more. These are absolutely correct—and key to motivating the employees! These are the actions which are not done in the seven failure situations. I build on the experts' teachings, explain why leaders do not do these things, and inspire leaders to develop perceptions and behaviors that lead to successful change initiatives.

---

* I recently came across an article by Bill Murphy Jr. which addresses some of my points: 7 Things Great Leaders Always Do (But Mere Managers Always Fear) from web 06/13/2014 http://www.inc.com/bill-murphy-jr/7-things-great-leaders-always-do-but-mere-managers-always-fear.html

Outline of this book

Prologue & Preface presents an event which started my thinking about change. It also tells why I ultimately wrote this book.

Chapter 1—Introduction (this chapter) discusses change and its effects on employees and leaders. It presents some approaches that others have used and my contribution. It shows how to get the most as you read.

Chapters 2 through 5 take you on a step by step journey to improve your odds of achieving the outcomes you want. Chapter 6 illustrates the way the ideas have worked, or not, in the real world. Chapter 7 returns to the seven ways change can fail and how to apply this book's approaches. Epilogue & Summary completes the opening story from the Prologue and sums up the key points of my solution.

Chapter 2—Getting Started—The YES I AM Solution. Here I explain the basic ideas of this book. ***YES I AM*** is an acronym to help you remember the key starting points. Using this model helps you come up with better ideas for your change, draw greater commitment from your employees and enjoy substantially better results than you may have expected. It ends by showing how you can manage your own uncertainty.

Some of the ideas here come from the wide array of published material. To help remember the tools, here is the acronym:

Your Passion	*you* must truly care about the gains from the change.
Everyone Benefits	everyone must see *their* benefits for true success.
Seek Their Ideas	*their* ideas will enhance yours.
Include Everyone	*they* will surprise you.
Ask for Help	*they* can actually do wonders if given the chance.
Manage Uncertainty	find ways to *feel* secure in the midst of the storm!

INTRODUCTION

You will explore these points and get tools to actually use them!

The **YES I AM Solution** is my version of many of the published approaches to the first phase of the change process. While there are new ideas here, I also include those of others who have come before me thus "standing on the shoulders of giants." [4] In presenting each point, I show how it may require working against your strong inclination to maintain control over the situation. Please don't let this "put you off." Hang in, and you will see how valuable these tools can be.

As you read, you will gain an understanding of why these ideas are often not used. Through the exercises and tasks I hope to make a compelling case for letting go of some of this control even though the process may feel very uncomfortable.

Remember, the **YES I AM solution** only covers the first phase of the change process. These ideas only serve to get you through the "Getting Started" phase. I hope you will try these methods and see for yourself that they are valuable.

Chapter 3—The Role of Control presents my ideas on how control, in the conventional understanding of the word, affects the change process. When leaders begin to understand the various aspects of motivation and empowerment, they often react negatively to letting go of power. This chapter provides an understanding of how rather than losing power, the leader actually becomes stronger with these tools.

The next two chapters will take you beyond the initial phase of change.

Chapter 4—Taking Steps Toward the Goal presents my interpretation of the literature on the next part of the change introduction. Here again, I will provide you with examples and exercises to bring the ideas home. We'll briefly discuss each of the elements essential for a complete, long-term, successful change process.

Chapter 5—Institutionalizing the Change is a critical part of the overall process. Do it inadequately and before long everything will revert to *how things used to be!*

Chapters 4 and 5 are not intended to be exhaustive or even complete; these sections simply point the way to the rest of the change management process.

Chapter 6—Change Examples: From Good to Awful shows you reality. Perhaps you would join the skeptics who say, "Ideas and concepts are fine; and exercises can be useful, but how do I know these ideas have worked in the real world?" Here are specific examples, many from the media, that demonstrate how the ideas in this book work and what happens when leaders neglect to use them.

In each example, I've linked the narrative to the model in *Chapter 2—Getting Started—The YES I AM Solution* to show how using or neglecting the tool contributed to success (or failure). Some stories will also relate to elements in Chapters 4 and 5.

Chapter 7—Change Failed? Not Yours! Here you return to the original question: Why don't leaders use these well-known tools? You will get to see examples for each of the seven sources of problems and how to get past your own barriers.

Here I will show how the *YES I AM Solution* (as well as the other tools) can be made to work for you.

Epilogue & Summary revisits the opening story and ties it in to the earlier parts of the book. Then I challenge you to follow the ideas and apply the *YES I AM Solution* to meet *your* needs.

How to get the most out of this book

You will be more convinced if you study the sample **situations** and try out the concepts in the "**mini-workshops.**" I've provided these situations with dialog for you to get a sense of how the tools are used so I call them workshops. My students have found these examples useful, and the workshop approach is intended to help you experience the tools and methods I am suggesting.

The **stories** and **situations** throughout the book are intended to bring some reality to the theory. Theory is often dull and leads the reader to

INTRODUCTION

think about the writer: "What does he know? Has he ever had to meet a deadline? Has he had to get work out when the customer is continually changing requirements?" See if you can imagine the situations and how you might feel in the shoes of each story's characters.

The "**mini-workshops**" give you the opportunity to practice the new skills. These exercises show you what actually happens when you use these tools. Since we are dealing with people, the key responses can be visceral as well as behavioral. And you will need to find your own way to use the tools.

There are three types of information and I have structured them to be easily identified.

1. The ideas, concepts and explanations are presented in this font.

2. Examples or demonstrations of the ideas are shown in this font. It is also used for dialog demonstrations of the ideas.

> 3. Many sections suggest tasks for you to do to help you learn the tools presented. Such material is presented indented and with a gray background such as here.

Blank pages are available for you to make notes as you read. These are headed:

[Your notes]

The ideas presented are based on my long career in industry. In retrospect, I found that I was doing the very things described by the leadership experts and getting outstanding results. The ideas of these experts are valuable, and I hope you will delve into these resources and also apply their wisdom to your change initiatives.

Before you read further, consider yourself. Do any of these situations seem familiar? Are you currently faced with any of them?
- You have an exciting new product to develop…
- Your division is losing market share…
- Production quality has been slipping…
- A competitor has suggested a merger…
- Your organization is launching a new approach to fund-raising …
- Receivables are very old…
- Inventory "turns" are too slow…
- Your management team has developed an aggressive new strategic plan…

Every one of these provides the opportunity for a significant gain for your organization and each will require changes which will affect many people. But as I've already pointed out, less than a third of these change initiatives will be successful. Keep your own situation in mind as you read. This book will help you succeed with *your* change initiatives.

If implementing all of the steps presented in this book feels overwhelming, work with one tool at a time. Each of the tools from Chapters 2 through 5 can be applied individually.

Chapter Two

GETTING STARTED— THE YES I AM SOLUTION

In this and the next three chapters, we'll take a closer look at the four principal parts of change management. This chapter teaches the six parts of the **YES I AM** model for initiating change. As we go through it, consider the question "Why don't leaders use this material?"

Some of the ideas here come from the wide array of published material. To help remember the tools, I am repeating the six-point acronym mentioned earlier—**YES I AM**:

Your Passion	*you* must truly care about the gains from the change.
Everyone Benefits	everyone must see *their* benefits for true success.
Seek Their Ideas	*their* ideas will enhance yours.
Include Everyone	*they* will surprise you.
Ask for Help	*they* can actually do wonders if given the chance.
Manage Uncertainty	find ways to *feel* secure in the midst of the storm!

Your Situation

I want you to really get what is here so I challenge you to relate it to something with which you are currently dealing. You may easily decide that this is obvious and you are getting it. My experience suggests that it is never that easy. You will need to practice the ideas to truly absorb and implement them.

Therefore, right now, think of a situation in which you currently need to achieve some specific objective and where other people will be affected by your actions. First, consider the desired outcomes: What do you want to achieve; what will be the important benefits? Make sure they are truly significant. Be certain that you care about the results.

Then think about the people who will be affected: What will happen to them? What will their concerns be?

I will call this "*Your Situation*," and we will return to it frequently. As you read the book, I will ask you to apply the ideas that we consider to *Your Situation*, the one you selected here!

I suggest that you make notes about your thoughts. The next page is placed here for your use; you will find such pages throughout the book.

So let's go to *Your Passion*

[Your notes]

GETTING STARTED—THE YES I AM SOLUTION

Your Passion

Passion and urgency often go together. When you realize that something is urgent and you care about it, you will become more passionate about it. Here are some examples.

Imagine that walls in the coffee-break room are painted a dreary brown. The people in your organization hang out there, and you think it would be nice if the place were more attractive.

But how urgent is the redecorating? Will it have much effect on operations? How much do you care about how the room looks? Will you fight to get it redecorated? Will your team be forever grateful for a nicer break room? Not very likely. No real passion here!

What about at home? Let's say you live in a tornado belt, and you don't have a shelter to protect your family. You have seen tornadoes destroy homes nearby. You are concerned about your family. You really want to protect them. Would you have some passion here?

How about in your company: You realize your company's raw materials inventory is very large, and the stock turns[*] are small. What could the company do with the cash tied up in inventory? For example: It could reduce your debt service which goes straight to the bottom line! Or, the savings could reduce the cost of finished goods. In either case, you could price your products more competitively and increase sales, having an even larger impact on the bottom line! If you use the savings in either way, the company benefits and you look like a hero!

Are you starting to feel some passion around these ideas?

Good!

---

[*] "Stock turns" and "inventory turnover" are accounting measures of the number of times inventory is sold or used in a time period such as a year. From the web at en.wikipedia.org/wiki/Inventory_turnover

How do passion and urgency drive the change process?

Let's work with the inventory system.

Introducing the new inventory system will be a difficult and probably expensive task; you had better be able to make a good case to get it approved. Because of the various groups you have to work with and possibly many vendors, you will need a lot of energy to keep going through the tough times.

Changing the inventory management system will affect many people: Certainly purchasing agents and inventory managers; how about the design engineers who may have to enter data about components? Production managers who need to get parts in the shop at the right time will definitely feel the impact; perhaps their delivery schedules will be missed. Or financial managers might be concerned about money tied up in inventory (that's where we began!).

How about that tornado!

It's heading this way, and the kids are outside—something needs to be done—and *now*! Go find the kids; get them inside; get them to a safe location!

Oh wait—you haven't planned for a safe location? Then let's back up a bit: You live in a tornado area, and last week a neighboring town got hit by a bad storm. What will you do when one is barreling down on *your* home? Do you think it might be a good idea to build a storm cellar? Now! Oh, you plan to outrun the storm? Did anyone in that nearby town successfully do that? Did they even try to do that? Where were their pieces found?

But it will cost a lot to build the cellar. You have a choice: storm cellar or Caribbean vacation? Caribbean vacation or storm cellar? Have some fun now, or save your family next year? Hmmm? Tough call?

You may realize that your storm cellar is an urgent need—you may even need it next week (I hope not).

You truly care about your family a lot. You really want to protect them.

So there you have it—but wait a minute! What does your wife or partner think? Perhaps he or she *really* wants to go to the Caribbean. And your kids? They may not care about the Caribbean, but they don't want you digging up their finished-cellar play area. And further, your partner doesn't want the finished basement touched either.

You have your urgent need, and you are passionate about it, but what can you do? Keep reading…

What we have done so far in *YES I AM*:

Your Passion   *you* must truly care about the gains from the change.

Task for right now

Remember *Your Situation*? Back on page 20 I asked you to think about a benefit that you really wanted. Why is it so important? What will happen if you do not get these results? Re-examine it. How do you feel about it? Do you really want that outcome? Is it really important to you that you achieve it? Are you willing to do the hard work to make it successful?

Take a moment and list three reasons you want to achieve the outcome you desire.

Really, *do it now*!

If you don't have several good reasons, perhaps this change is not urgent enough. If that is the case, go back and select something else as *Your Situation*.

[Your notes]

GETTING STARTED—THE YES I AM SOLUTION

Everyone Benefits

The change you seek must be urgent and very important or it won't succeed. You are convinced of the importance and urgency, so you announce that there will be a change in the inventory control system. You explain why it is important for the company to reduce inventory. From your employees' responses, you know that they get it. Yet no one is stepping up and trying to help!

Why is it so hard to get people to move? To get them to do what you are asking?

One problem is that they don't see the payoff for *themselves*. They don't see how these changes will benefit them directly. Instead they see how it may be trouble for them.

You are asking them to do new things which might prove too difficult. They must learn new skills which may be too hard to learn. And most of all, these changes may make them obsolete—their very jobs may be at risk! All they can see are the risks.

How can you expect people overwhelmed by such worries to get excited about your change?

They are asking:

What's in it for me?

Is there something about the proposed change which will benefit your employees? Do they know what that is? Do you think that they are even *thinking* about how it could be good for them?

Scott Keller and Carolyn Aiken wrote a compelling article called "The Inconvenient Truth About Change Management—Why it isn't working and what to do about it." They pointed out that there are many ways that the employees can benefit from changes, but you are not the best one to tell them what those benefits are. Keller and Aiken call it their Inconvenient Truth #2: While it is necessary for your employees to benefit from the change, the inconvenient truth is that you will do best by "listening and not telling." Get your employees to figure out their benefits for themselves. [5]

Keller and Aiken suggest the benefits of a change may serve five stakeholders:
- The company
- Society
- Customers
- The working team, and
- Me (the leader or employee), personally.

Keller and Aiken are saying that you must listen and work with your employees to help them find their own benefits.

Consider these water cooler conversations:

> "Did you hear? Joe was just laid off—for no good reason."
> "He seemed to be in the wrong place at the wrong time."
> "I don't get it. He is one of our best. We'll hurt without him."

Or:

> "They want me to learn to use the new ERP system. I don't even know what ERP is. I'm too old to learn some fancy new software. I guess I better start checking Monster.com."
> "Come on. Don't give up so fast. You'll catch on."
> "Look what happened to Joe—and he's a better engineer than I am."

These employees are probably not going to try to figure out the ways this change will benefit them. It is up to you to help everyone see how they will benefit directly or indirectly. Get them passionate about it. But it's difficult to inspire passion when trying to present all of Keller and Aiken's five stakeholders—the company and four others: the employee, the working team, the customers, and society.

One of your first tasks must be getting them to see the benefits which *they* will value; if you don't, you will be facing an uphill fight. With them understanding *their* possible gains, you are more likely to get their support!

Example of how you might approach *Everyone Benefits*:

> As the leader, you say: "I realize that changing the inventory system is sudden and may be unnerving. You might be very concerned."
>
> Employees may think: *You bet I'm concerned. If this works out, I'll get laid off. Who needs this?*
>
> Anticipating their response, you continue:
>
> You say: "I have only told you why the company needs to do this. But there will be benefits for you and the other employees too.
>
> "Your work will be easier since the parts you need will always be available when you and your team need them. Any special instructions will be provided along with the parts.
>
> "And since this will be creating more profit for the company, we will be sharing that with every team that helps make it happen.
>
> "What would you like to see happen here?"

You might go on to suggest other possible employee benefits: They may get special recognition or they may value that the company is improving the environment and becoming a better community citizen.

Be sure to give them a chance to tell you what *they* think about the plan, how they are feeling.

Give them time to say whatever they wish. Help them better understand their gains.

If they challenge you with other complaints, listen. Don't try to explain away their concerns. If you can give clear responses that truly remove their worries, do so. If not, promise to explore what might be done and get back to them promptly with answers.

You want the employees to want to help make the change a success for themselves as well as the company. Find your own way to help them get there.

When the news isn't all good (possible layoffs, salary cuts, factory closings), you could feel overwhelmed, become a dictator or make mistakes. You will fail to get the most out of your change initiative. You will miss the opportunities which could substantially help you succeed. Your employees may even be able to provide those ideas. Consider this as you read the next section, **Seek Their Ideas**.

What we have done so far in *YES I AM*:

Your Passion   *you* must truly care about the gains from the change.

Everyone Benefits   everyone must see *their* benefits for true success.

Task for right now

Back to *Your Situation*: *You* know why you want the change, but from the employees' point of view, why will they want it? Can you help them see how *they* will benefit?

Looking over the five beneficiaries/stakeholders (above, p. 27), the list includes Company, Team, and Personal. Right now, for *Your Situation*, come up with ways the other two, Society and your Customer, will benefit.

GETTING STARTED—THE YES I AM SOLUTION

> Write down the reasons that members of your team will want *Your Situation* resolved successfully. Remember to consider these reasons from *their* possible four points of view: Team, Personal, Societal and Customer.

[Your notes]

SEEK THEIR IDEAS

Many leaders are surprised to learn that their employees actually know more about their work than the leaders do. Employees often understand the details differently and better than others—even the original designers! This can be true even in highly technical areas.

Workers on the front lines do their tasks day in and day out, so they know what works and what causes them difficulties. They can tell you what equipment is most reliable and what software is easiest to use. They can also tell you what fails most often, what takes the most effort to use, what tires them out, what causes delays, and what causes the most accidents.

They know what information is hard to find, which data entry modes give trouble, and which ones work smoothly.

Employees also know what your customers complain about, and what they really like.

In short, they often know more about the work than their leaders.

For example, maintenance workers on airplanes know more about improving maintenance than the engineers who designed the plane! [16] When it was necessary to reduce costs at American Airlines, it was the frontline workers who figured out how to do it. (See **American Airlines Maintenance Operations**, p. 82)

When you are about to make a change in your organization, first talk with your employees. Remember that you, the leader, need your employees to want this change to be a success. Be sure you help them see how **Everyone Benefits** (including them!). Then seek your employees' help to make the change not be just a success, but a *great* success. Tell them about your ideas and ask them to help make your plan even better.

Asking for help from your employees may feel like you are not doing your job. *You* are the boss; you are supposed to know what needs to be done. Asking them feels like relinquishing some of your control. Yes, I am asking you to give up this control, some of your power. It is very common to want to control any situation when you are feeling uncertain or concerned. Yet because you want them to *want* to make the change successful, you *must* involve them.

Even if you are certain that you know how to manage the change, ask for ideas anyway. You may be surprised at what you get. Being open to making changes in your plan can make it even better. Consider this scenario:

Example of how you might approach *Seek Their Ideas*

Suppose you have called a department meeting.

You, as the leader, say: "We have a problem: We need to improve the materials management situation in the production shop. As I see it, our raw material costs are killing our competitive advantage. If we don't reduce our raw materials inventory, our costs will erode our profit margin. And our organization will be in big trouble."

Employees are thinking: *Sure, but what does that have to do with me? Maybe you could pay me more and I'd work longer hours to save some money—sure!*

You say: "You may be thinking 'What's this got to do with me?'

"Well, we are considering buying a new inventory management system, but I am not sure I know enough to get all the benefits that it could provide."

Employees think: *You are right about that. You know zilch about the inventory system. You probably never even visited the warehouse.*

You say: "You know how it presently works—or doesn't work—and you know where it needs to be improved.

"I would like to hear what you think. Please consider this and give me your ideas. I want this to be a significant improvement. With your ideas I think it will be."

You pause and then say: "As you consider this, I hope you will want to help make the plan better."

Here the leader is telling them his/her ideas and asking for theirs. In the process, you **Include Everyone** and prepare them for you to **Ask for Help**—covered a bit further on in the **Solution**.

If you were an employee in this situation, you would have a range of feelings and thoughts. Perhaps you feel on the spot; perhaps you think you are being tricked. You wonder what the leader really wants from you.

You might feel confused; no one has ever asked your opinion on anything important.

Perhaps you feel pleased—pleased to be acknowledged and asked for your ideas.

Now assume that one of your employees made a suggestion.

> You (the leader) say: "I like some of your ideas a lot, and I want to use them. Here is how I see your idea about… fitting in with the…. Did I correctly understand you?
>
> "Did anyone help you with this idea? I would like to be sure they also get credit."

You might suggest some changes to parts of their ideas. You might also discover that some of the ideas came from the employee's colleagues when he or she discussed this matter with them. Be sure to give the others the credit they deserve.

And now, if you were the employee, how do you feel?

In most cases, you are going to feel important, valued, and (perhaps most of all) empowered! Aren't you going to want to help as much as you can? Aren't you going to want to do more than is expected? Don't you want this to be a success as much as your boss does?

When you are the leader and change initiator, please remember how this process feels to the employee. Look for ways to seek ideas from your team. Where you can, add their ideas to your plan. Sometimes this will feel uncomfortable: *This is my plan; how can I let others change it?*

Can you think about it this way? You have developed a plan on how to achieve a goal, one that is important, one you are passionate about. If the goal can be achieved in a more efficient or somehow better method than your original plan, that's a good thing, isn't it?

If leaders can give up control of the methods of achieving goals, they can allow for better changes to be implemented and better goals to be achieved.

Yes, it is uncomfortable, but don't let this discomfort stop you from using good ideas. You and your company will both benefit from these new ideas.

And don't forget to let your employees know that you value their contributions.

Remember, when your project succeeds, you succeed—no matter where the idea originated or who did the work.

What we have done so far in *YES I AM*:

Your Passion — *you* must truly care about the gains from the change.

Everyone Benefits — everyone must see *their* benefits for true success.

Seek Their Ideas — *their* ideas will enhance yours.

Task for right now

Back to *Your Situation*. Let's start small. Think of one person in your group to approach for ideas; let's call him Jim. Find a time to explain *Your Situation* to him. Answer his questions—completely! Then ask him what he thinks.

As you listen, try to understand what he is saying and try to discern his thinking behind it. Only ask questions to clarify points.

No matter what Jim says, *don't say anything negative.* When you understand, whether you agree or not, tell him that you will consider his ideas, and then do so.

Afterwards, recall how it went. Did he provide any ideas at all? Did you like them? Any of them? Think about how you felt. Were you totally comfortable or were you somewhat nervous? When did you feel most at ease, and what was the hardest to do?

What occurred just as you expected, and when were you surprised by the result?

Keep thinking about this. We will come back to it.

Are you ready to speak with a second person? If so, go for it.

Another way to do this would be in a group meeting. Here you would ask the group members for ideas to improve the plan. Discuss any that arise right there and show respect for the idea and the person making the suggestion. Do not dismiss any idea, and promise to consider each one.

GETTING STARTED—THE YES I AM SOLUTION

> Later return to the group and tell them what ideas you will be using. Along the way, you might discuss specific ideas with the originators. Handle those conversations in the same way as you would approach an individual for his or her input.
>
> We will continue this discussion later in the Ask for Help section.

[Your notes]

INCLUDE EVERYONE

"Now, wait a minute!" you might say. "Leaders are in charge; they know what must be done and are supposed to tell the employees what to do—right?"

Think about how much information you currently share with your employees. Do you tell them about company news which may not even be related to your current change initiative? How about the status of physical office moves, a new marketing program, possible re-organization, possible bonuses? Or do you think, "Why do they need to know that?" When you tell them such things, employees feel much more valued.

Think about a boss you have had who largely ignored your thoughts and ideas, told you what to do, and made sure you did just that. At that time, were you glad to come in each morning? Was your work exciting or even interesting? Did you want to make a success of your project, your boss or the company?

Now think about another boss. This one asked your advice, discussed problems with you, was pleased to use your ideas, told you what was going on, treated you as a valuable member of the team, and perhaps asked you to take a leading role in a project. Does that change your answers to the questions in the last paragraph—coming in each day, interesting work, wanting to make work successful?

Compare and contrast your feelings in each case.

I imagine that you would want to help the second boss, an inspirational leader, achieve his or her objectives, wouldn't you?

You can be that kind of Leader and get your employees to respond to you like the boss in the second example.

Examples of how you might *Include Everyone*

First example

Suppose that you are the leader and have already been getting ideas from your employees as described earlier. You are feeling pretty good about it so consider this:

One day Sandra stops by your office.
> She says: "I heard that sales are down, and management is worried. What's going on?"

You know about this; there *is* a serious problem in the company's market. You are not sure whether to tell Sandra what is happening or deny the situation.

Many leaders will try to limit the amount of information which is shared with the employee. These leaders might deny that there is a problem or, having acknowledged the problem, might minimize its importance.

They think: *why does the employee need to know any more than that?*

Does this sound like you or anyone you know?

Another type of leader will think: Is there an important reason to withhold this information? If not, sharing may be valuable.

It is rare in my experience that withholding information is actually necessary. However, many leaders still share very little.

Second example

You are walking past Felix, one of your technicians.
> Felix says: "You know, I have been thinking about this system design and I have an idea."
>
> He launches into his idea.
>
> You listen politely for a while and then You say: "I'm glad you have been thinking about this; however, please continue with the current design."

How do you think Felix feels? How would you feel if you were Felix? Ignored? Dismissed? Even put down?

> On the other hand, after hearing Felix's idea you might instead say: "I'm glad you have been thinking about this; I'd like to better understand it. I don't have the time right now, so please come to my office in the morning and tell me more about your idea."

Often the idea is not new, except to the employee. You may already know the idea is not suitable or feasible, but honoring the employee is important as a motivator. However, you will have to explain why the idea is not workable in a way that invites future ideas.

There are times where certain employees have what seem to be an excessive number of ideas—too many for you to handle. In these cases, mentoring is necessary to help them learn how to better evaluate their ideas before presenting them to you or others.

You, the leader, want to get all possible good ideas, you want to involve all of your employees, and you want them to believe that you actually value them as part of your team—because you do!

What we have done so far in *YES I AM*:

Your Passion	*you* must truly care about the gains from the change.
Everyone Benefits	everyone must see *their* benefits for true success.
Seek Their Ideas	*their* ideas will enhance yours.
Include Everyone	*they* will surprise you.

Task for right now

Again back to *Your Situation*.

Get your direct-reports together. First tell them that you realize that you have not always kept them aware of the activities. Since you do value their thoughts, you will now, regularly, give them updates. Then tell them what is going on in the company

If you have not done this before—or it has been a while since the last such meeting—you may find that only a few will speak up. Give them plenty of time. Some may ask many questions; don't cut them off. They may be asking the very questions that others are thinking. As you answer, direct your words around the group; do not give your answer just to the person who asked.

Going forward, you can use other communications such as email, banners, occasionally meetings and the like. You don't need to have frequent big meetings.

Some leaders find meetings like this tedious but they are critical to keeping everyone involved. These meetings are just the beginning in building an inclusive employee group.

In the next section we'll look at ways to get even more help from your team members, *Ask for Help*.

[Your notes]

GETTING STARTED—THE YES I AM SOLUTION

ASK FOR HELP

Ideas and suggestions from your employees have been great. Your plan has been improved, and your employees are feeling better about themselves. How about asking them to do more—to actually do jobs they suggested?

Remember Jim (back in **Seek Their Ideas** p. 35)? Let's say he made a useful suggestion. Go back to him and ask him to actually implement his suggestion. Give him the necessary authority and resources.

Whoa! Now I'm asking you to really give up control! You're not so sure about that, are you? This is even more risky than asking for ideas. With ideas you can still control what happens; you can use them or change them. You are still making the decisions.

Remember that you may not have expected your employees to be helpful in the planning. Their response and ideas surprised and pleased you.

When you think about asking them for help, you worry that they may not be able to work independently, to do some of the more important tasks. Again, they will surprise you!

People like to know that they are important. When they see that you value them, they want to please you, to prove that your trust is well founded. How much can you allow yourself to trust them?

When you hired your employees, you thought that they were capable people. They no doubt are, so give them things which will take advantage of those capabilities. Trust that they will come through.

In the next section, **Manage Uncertainty**, I will help you with your concerns. But for now, stay with me on this point.

Example of how you might *Ask for Help*

Suppose Jason is a member of your group, and he gave you a great idea at the last meeting. A week later you see him:

> You (Jason's supervisor) say: "You know that I liked your idea and we added it to the plan."

Jason thinks: *I'm glad he liked my idea. The plan will definitely work better, and I'm excited that I have helped.*

You say: "Now I want you to actually make that happen. I want you to carry out the idea you suggested. Are you interested?"

Jason thinks: *I bet he will get me started and then micromanage me at every step; Or perhaps, others won't listen to me because I'm not the boss. Or...(you fill in the blank).*

You say: "You seem hesitant; what are you thinking about?"

Jason may take a risk and say: "Look, no one will take me seriously. After all, I'm just a technician (or you fill in the blank). Also, how much time will you give me to complete the task? What are the boundaries?

"Will you really let me do it my way?"

You say: "Please lay out a plan for what you think is necessary to get the job done. I will review it with you and when we agree, I will give you the authority to do the job.

"Does that help?"

Imagine how Jason is feeling: concerned, maybe nervous?

Jason is thinking: *What have I gotten myself into?*

You say: "You still seem hesitant; how can I help you?

"Please continue to tell me your concerns. Discuss them with me and let's see what happens. Perhaps you can get to thinking, *I can't wait to get started; this is so exciting!*"

Now, as the leader, wouldn't you like to have all of your team members feel that way?

On the other hand, as the leader, you may be feeling exactly like your employee, Jason: concerned and/or nervous; and thinking: *What have I gotten myself into? Can I trust Jason to do the job?*

Please hold that feeling and see how the next section **Manage Uncertainty** addresses it.

Asking for help

Alan's Story

Here is how Alan, a former student, dealt with his situation: Alan was a new supervisor. He realized it was necessary to collect data about his operation from the employees. When he had some opposition, he decided to ask the employees for their help. Several had suggestions. Alan gave the task to the person who had good ideas but was the strongest opponent of the changes. The results exceeded Alan's expectations! The details are in Alan's Story, *Chapter 6— Change Examples: From Good to Awful—Successful Changes* (p. 87).

What we have done so far in YES I AM:

Your Passion	*you* must truly care about the gains from the change.
Everyone Benefits	everyone must see *their* benefits for true success.
Seek Their Ideas	*their* ideas will enhance yours.
Include Everyone	*they* will surprise you.
Ask for Help	*they* can actually do wonders if given the chance.

Task for right now

Now for *Your Situation*: Whom can you ask to take on a task? Look at the possible tasks.

For example, a project often has both critical tasks (without which the project will fail), and non-critical "nice-to-have" tasks. You would like to see these non-critical tasks done, but their absence would not be the end of the world. You might offer one of the "nice-to-haves" to a new, untested member of the group. Give this person full control of the task, and step out of the way. Don't disappear; remain available to help if the employee wants assistance. Check how things are going, so the employee knows you care about the task. When your employee is successful, everyone wins. If it doesn't work out, you have learned something about the employee's capabilities without jeopardizing your project. As such a task progresses you may have the opportunity to mentor the employee. The company and the employee benefit!

On the other hand, if the "nice-to-have" task is interesting, one of your more experienced employees might want to do it. That person may say "Hey, you gave that task to the new person. Why didn't you offer it to me?" Think about this before you offer the task. This could be a good time to experiment. Instead of offering it to a specific person make it available to anyone as an "extra," an interesting task to be done in addition to their regular task. It might be a way to try letting your team select their work.

GETTING STARTED—THE YES I AM SOLUTION

In any of these cases, consider how you will feel if things go wrong: Angry? Annoyed? Betrayed? What else? Make a list of these feelings.

Now think about what you will do in each of these cases. Will you be able to pick up the pieces? Will you be able to survive? Will you be okay even if things go wrong?

Really consider these questions. Then develop strategies that will allow you to cope, successfully, with any situation that occurs. For each feeling on your list, answer these questions and plan your responses to each. Be tough on yourself.

You only need to be sure that you will be *okay*, not perfectly fine.

Take each concern in turn and satisfy yourself that you know you will be okay regardless of how it goes.

One rule: Find ways to be okay *without taking over control*, unless there *really* is no alternative.

Make notes about all of your thoughts in this **Task for right now**.

Before you take the actions suggested here, actually asking someone to take on a task, read the next part, **Manage Uncertainty**. This will solidify your confidence. When you are ready, you can return to this part and get your employee's help.

[Your notes]

GETTING STARTED—THE YES I AM SOLUTION

MANAGE UNCERTAINTY

When you realize that things could be much better than they are, you begin to seek ways to make that happen. You really want to succeed in making this change, but you realize that doing the *E, S, I,* and *A* parts of **YES I AM** requires taking some risks. To involve your employees means giving up control over them. Many leaders are uncomfortable with this risk.

Leaders have to deal with risks if they are to achieve their ends. We as leaders must find ways to make those risks tolerable.

Example of how to *Manage Uncertainty*

The first time I had to deal with managing a change, I was concerned that I might not be able to make it work. There were so many elements which were unknowns; how was I going to be able to pull it all together?

For me the biggest challenge was trusting that the members of my team would deliver. I did not want to "micromanage" them and yet I needed some security.

What worked for me was to add the "right" controls to the mix.

When I offered a task to one of my team, Kathy, here is how I did it:

> I said: "Kathy you showed interest in the laser drive task. I would like you to do it. You have my full authority to get it done and I will back you 100 percent!. You won't have to get my explicit approval for each action. Do the job as you see fit! Are you interested?"
>
> Kathy said: "Of course!"
>
> I said: "Great! Now I need two things from you: First agree to meet with me regularly every two weeks so I can see how things are progressing. (Choose an appropriate interval for your project.) And second: Promise to inform me immediately if a problem arises even if you believe that you will be able to handle it."

Delegating full authority is essential, even though it can be very uncomfortable for the leader. My comfort comes from the two extra requirements: meeting regularly and the promise to alert me.

These two agreements allowed me sleep at night—well, most nights—until I knew things were truly working!

Now check yourself: Do you really care if you get the benefits desired? Does it matter all that much? Do you want this more than anything? If not, go back to **Your Passion.** You must truly care about the gains from the change.

Then ask yourself the following: Are you willing to take the risk of allowing your employees to do their best? Can you trust *yourself* to be able to handle any surprises? If not, perhaps you are not ready to achieve all that is possible!

We have completed all elements in *YES I AM*:

Your Passion	*you* must truly care about the gains from the change.
Everyone Benefits	everyone must see *their* benefits for true success.
Seek Their Ideas	*their* ideas will enhance yours.
Include Everyone	*they* will surprise you.
Ask for Help	*they* can actually do wonders if given the chance.
Manage Uncertainty	find ways to *feel* secure in the midst of the storm!

Task for right now

Now that you have satisfied yourself that you will be okay, go back to the end of the *Ask for Help* section (back on page 46). Speak with the person who you were going to ask for help, and offer the task.

Suppose the employee provided a good idea, you might say, "I would like you to implement it. Would you like to?"

"Of course I would!"

Then ask, "What would you like from me?" If at all possible, promise to provide what is needed.

Then describe what *you* want to feel comfortable. Perhaps your needs are similar to what I described above. Whether they are or not, ask for what you want clearly and specifically.

If the employee declines, you have several alternatives:
- You could gently encourage the employee; *gently* is key. You want the employee to want to do the task.
- You could ask "What would you like to do; is there another part of the project which is more appealing."
- The employee may say "I don't want to make the choice, please tell me what you would like me to do."

In the last case, the employee is actually telling you what he or she wants. This book is all about getting people to do what they want (and to want what you want). You have now been told, so do what you have been asked. I expect that you will be pleased with the result.

And you are off. Good luck!

[Your notes]

Chapter Three

THE ROLE OF CONTROL

Before discussing the four intermediate steps that will help you accomplish your goal (Chapter 4), I will discuss the controversial issue of control. You may be asking these questions: "Where does control fit in?" "Isn't it the leader's job to control everything?" Here is how it applies.

Control has three meanings in business.

1. Traditionally, *control* means telling your employees exactly what to do, and then monitoring them. You make certain that they do what you directed and nothing else. This type of control—which is very common—greatly limits project or business success, because it inhibits employees' freely given contributions.
2. *Control* may also refer to measures you use to ensure getting your desired results. It entails establishing SMART [6] goals* and measuring the outcomes. This control comes by comparing what you get with what you want and then making adjustments to correct the outcome. This form of control gets the desired results.
3. An unexpected form of control is *actually letting go of control.* You can build this kind of control on the second (goal-setting) type, and it can lead to getting even more than you were seeking. Letting go of control motivates people to excel.

Giving **over** control is not giving **up** control!

You might ask, "Isn't that a big risk? How can I be sure my employees will really do what needs to be done?"

---

* SMART: Specific, Measureable, Attainable, Relevant, and Time-bound.

THE ROLE OF CONTROL

You're right; there is a big risk here, but you also face a risk when you make decisions on your own. Can you be certain that what you're telling them is best? Letting go of traditional "control" potentially yields greater benefits: You will be tapping into the collective wisdom of the people who actually do the work day-to-day.

In his paper "Control in Organizations: Individual Adjustment and Organizational Performance," Arnold S. Tannenbaum further explains these ideas and provides compelling supporting data. [7]

Example of Traditional Control Methods

Here is a traditional way to introduce a change:

Sol, the leader of a large printing operation, walked into a meeting he scheduled with his shop's union leaders.

> Sol said: "You know why we are here. Our company is in trouble, and we need to reduce the time to do full-scale maintenance on our large machines.
>
> "I have put together this list of the maintenance tasks starting with paper-roll-mounting handlers and ending with the folding and cutting operations.
>
> "I have asked the manufacturer to send several engineers here to help. They will show you how each task must be improved.
>
> "I realize that cost reduction is not something you have been asked to do before. However, I'm sure you understand how important it is to the company, so I hope you will help cut the costs in half.
>
> "We have three months to completely revamp the maintenance process. We will meet every Monday morning at nine to see where we stand.
>
> "Any questions?
>
> "Okay, let's do it!"

Do you see how this leader used the **YES I AM Solution**? Of course, you don't! He didn't use it!

But we *can* use the **YES I AM Solution** to analyze why Sol did not get nearly the results he could have.

One might imagine the result: The change process took four months (which was too long) and two of the best employees left the company. The cost savings were only about 20 percent.

Sol's approach also might have created problems with the union since, typically, unions and management have difficulty working together. His changes might have idled some workers as the amount of work decreased. In that case, Sol would reduce head count which could lead to union grievances and possibly a strike.

Not exactly a great result!

Analysis

Let's now compare what Sol did with what might have been done using the *YES I AM Solution*. We will take each point:

Your Passion. Sol may have been passionate, so let's give him that, although it did not come through all that well in his short speech.

Everyone Benefits. Wait a minute; has Sol any idea what the employees will get from the change? Has he considered what anyone is feeling or thinking? Do the team members care about the project? Are they able to do what has been assigned to them? Are they concerned about whether there is any reason to do this except, perhaps, to make Sol happy? Perhaps they're thinking, *It's just management asking us to work harder.*

How would you answer these questions about Sol's proposed change?
- Is everyone going to benefit?
- Why is it important that they all benefit?

Assuming the company actually *might* close its doors, this project has the potential to help the employees keep their jobs. The idea of the union members working with management may have been a new idea, but the members have the opportunity to gain some real benefits, if management handles it well.

No one in this company has done this before; perhaps it is not possible. Is everyone going to be excited about this project or will they be

THE ROLE OF CONTROL

worried? With suitable employee and union benefits, they might be both, excited *and* worried. But at least they have a possible benefit.

Since Sol didn't show the employees the benefits for them, they will just have to buck up and do it. For example, in the AOL/Time-Warner merger the top management simply told them, make it work (see page 93.) As you may know, this merger failed!

On the other hand, can we find ways to give the employees some personal benefits besides keeping their jobs? Perhaps the change can create an improvement in the local community?

Sol was not looking for these benefits at all.

Seek Their Ideas. I guess Sol didn't do this either. Well, that's okay—at least it would be okay in a traditional control approach. After all, Sol has given the project a lot of thought and is sure the employees won't be able to add anything. Maybe he doesn't need to get their input on this. Besides, he has engineers from the manufacturer coming in to show them all how to run things. Many leaders would think that this is all that is necessary.

Remember that list of maintenance tasks for the equipment? How does Sol know that it's complete? Is it the correct set of tasks? Why *not* ask for their ideas. Sol might say to them: "Have I included everything? What do you think?"

It is remarkable how often workers know about problems or opportunities that the boss does not. And even if the boss learns nothing additional from the employees, honestly asking can add to the good feelings of the employees and increase their cooperation. Asking "honestly" implies a sincere intent to act on their answers when possible.

Include Employees. Since each person had a task, you might say that they were included. Do you think Sol's employees felt part of the process? They were not being kept informed about the program. They didn't know the full reasons for the program. How invested would you be if you were one of his employees?

Ask for Help. Sol may have thought he did. He made assignments and asked the employees to do them. Well, actually he told them—he did not ask.

While he may have created a good set of tasks for cost reduction, his workers may actually be better able to lead these improvements themselves. If so, perhaps he won't need the manufacturer's engineers, after all!

Manage Uncertainty. Sol has clearly laid out all of the tasks—there is no uncertainty. All of the employees will do their tasks, and at the end there will be a working revised maintenance system.

Since Sol made the assignments, he is sure that there won't be any problems, isn't he? Sol's certainty is dependent on everyone doing exactly what he directed. If someone is not doing as directed, Sol will remind them, forcefully if necessary.

> Notice the "hidden" uncertainty here. The assumption is that Sol has thought of everything! Nothing has escaped his thorough analysis. But *has* he thought of everything? Can *anyone* do this? Of course not; therefore, an element of uncertainty is part of every situation. The tools of this section are important in any change situation.

If Sol does choose to allow some of the employees to lead tasks as the model recommends, he *won't* be certain how things will turn out and he *will* become uncomfortable. That's when it becomes important to *Manage Uncertainty.* Check that part of the *YES I AM Solution.*

Again, remember that union workers rarely (if ever) help management solve a problem. The approach described below has actually worked with unions!

Example of the *YES I AM Solution* for dealing with control

Let's go back and run this scenario another way. In this version, *you* know something about the change process and the **YES I AM Solution**. Imagine that you are the leader of the group and you are introducing this change.

You, as the leader (not Sol), walked into the meeting with the shop union leaders.

THE ROLE OF CONTROL

You say: "You know why we are here. Our company is in trouble, and we need to reduce the time to do full-scale maintenance on our large machines. I'm very concerned and think that by working together we can make this happen.(**Your Passion**)

"The maintenance costs are seriously hurting our business. So, while the company will gain a lot from our success in reducing these costs, all of *us* will also benefit too. I'm going to tell you just how that can work."

Some of your employees may be suspicious.

Union leaders think: *Management will want us to cut our benefits and vacation. How's that going to be good for me?*

You say: "I want the union leaders to become part of the maintenance management team. You will be part of every key decision we make."

Union leaders think: *Sure, right!*

You say: "There will be no reduction in employees when you are successful. And, everyone in the union will also get recognition and perhaps rewarded for this success." **(Everyone Benefits)**

You ask: "What do you think about this?"

A union's strength is based on its number of members; retaining workers is very important. There may be some questions but this is looking good.

Also remember there are a number of other ways your employees might benefit. Suggest some of these as they might apply for your case. (Personal, societal, environmental…)

You let them see your enthusiasm and show them the importance to the company:

Let them suggest their own ideas for benefits that they would value; why each person would particularly value the success of the project. Explore their ideas and questions; discuss other possible benefits with the group.

Allow the discussion to play out for a while to see how they are feeling about it. Let them ask questions, and answer them truthfully, even the tough questions.

When they seem content for now, move on:

> You say: "I have put together this list of the maintenance tasks starting with paper-roll-mounting handlers and ending with the folding and cutting operations.
>
> "This was my best try, but I would like your help. Ask your union members to help make sure we are not missing something. Let's make this list as good as possible.
>
> "What do we need to add? What should be changed? Don't worry about feasibility just now; get everything on the list that may be necessary." **(Seek Their Ideas.)**

Be clear: You truly want their ideas to make the plan as good as it can be.

This may take a considerable amount of time. On a large project, it could take weeks or more. It is a critical task and must not be short-changed.

This is the planning phase of the project, and the planning phase can determine its overall success. Do this well now, and you will save much more time later when you don't have to retrace your steps after false starts.

When the task list is fairly stable, that is, it has not changed much *recently*, it is time to get the project moving. At a meeting you show that you want to move on.

> You say: "I realize that cost reduction is not something you have been asked to do before. However, you already gave us good ideas to help the project so I hope you will look for more ways that will result in still further cost reductions.
>
> "I am not going to bring in the manufacturer's engineers; I am sure that your members know more about what needs to be done anyway. Please have your members identify all the areas which can be improved and made more efficient.
>
> "Also, see who among your members (the employees) would like to lead some of the tasks. I would like help from as many as possible. This could mean dividing tasks but I think it would yield better results.

THE ROLE OF CONTROL

> "As you identify opportunities for improvement, let us know what you will need to do the job: equipment, money, and other resources. To be successful, you must have what you need and, to help you, I need to know what that is."

You have reminded them that they have provided new ideas and that you valued that. This is drawing them in; you are including them in the process. (**Include Employees**)

And you are showing even more trust: You have asked them to take ownership of their part of the project when you **Ask for Help**.

This could come together quickly, or it may take some time. Again, it is a vital part of getting the benefits you want. When you have the key tasks selected by your employees, you pull the project together.

> You say: "We have three months to completely revamp the maintenance process. I know that will be tight. We will meet every Monday morning at nine to see where we stand. Is that too often?
>
> "In addition, here is what I need from you: At any time, if something is not going as planned, don't wait for the meeting, come see me immediately and let's get it fixed.
>
> "Are you all okay with this?"

Even if checking up on progress were not necessary, hold occasional meetings to let everyone know how things are going. It costs little, and the involvement will pay off. Again, you are seeking their participation in the project management.

This describes what you need for your comfort while reinforcing the value of the employees and the union. And that's where the old notion of *control* comes in. Regular meetings and the employees' commitment to seek help when needed assure you that the project is moving forward. (**Manage Uncertainty**)

With this approach, this project might take only 11 weeks because the employees really want it to succeed. Typically, the cost savings could start at 40% and grow to 60% in a few months. Also employees' suggestions could also improve the production process to reduce through-put time by 10%. In the six months following the project, total grievances could go from thirteen to one. Admittedly, this is hypothetical but real-world experience shows these kinds of results.

Now look at how the **YES I AM Solution** has worked to provide the control the traditional leader wants.

You have the passion; you get **Everyone** on board; **Seek** their ideas; **Include** them all; **Ask** for their help, and **Manage** a system that keeps you sane.

The center four points of the model—**E, S, I and A**—build your employees' interest in, and commitment to the project. By having them help build the project details, you are getting them to have "skin in the game." By giving them authority to do their tasks, you are *empowering* them.

This gives you "control" over the project in a way that gets everyone to want to help.

You'll see a real-world example of how these principles worked for **American Airlines Maintenance Operations** described on p. 82.

Task for right now

Think about **Your Situation** and think about where you may have the greatest concern. That is, what aspects might you *really* want to control. It may be technical; for example, a tool or application may not be able to do what you need. It may be that you are considering allowing a person you do not know very well to take charge of a project. It may be that you are worried that there is not enough time to complete the project.

Makes some notes about the specific difficulties that you imagine may occur.

Next, for each difficulty, think of several ways you can help yourself to feel okay *without taking over control!* This may be hard to do.

How about using some of the **YES I AM Solution** steps? You might **Seek Their Ideas** regarding your areas of concern. Or you might **Include Everyone** in a discussion of how to make things work. You can try any of the steps.

Decide now how you will approach your specific project.

[Your notes]

Chapter Four

TAKING STEPS TOWARD THE GOAL

In *Chapter 2—Getting Started—The YES I AM Solution,* I showed you how to begin the process of improving your organization—making change work. But these suggestions are only the beginning steps; you have more to do before you're finished. This chapter will outline the next things you must do.

Don't be fooled by the lack of depth in this chapter. I cannot stress enough how important this section is for long-term success. As you approach this part of your project, seek additional guidance from other writers.

Rather than re-writing the book on Change Management, this section draws on the wealth of material already out there. The ideas presented here are similar to those of John Kotter's Eight Stage Process [8]. His eight points are Urgency, Guiding Coalition, Vision, Communicating the Vision, Empowering Employees, Short-Term Wins, Consolidating Gains, and Anchoring the Changes in the Culture. I structure the stages differently, but his ideas have been central to my thinking. These sections will not be comprehensive; Kotter and others have already done that effectively. My purpose is to give you some preliminary guidance.

Here, as in *Chapter 2—Getting Started—The YES I AM Solution,* you will find some **Tasks for right now** which will help you to understand each point and help you move forward toward your objectives. As you read, consider how to apply the tasks to **Your Situation**, the opportunity that you thought about in The *YES I AM Solution* on page 20.

63

FORM A SUPPORTIVE COMMITTEE

It will often be valuable to have a supportive group of colleagues dedicated to the success of the project. Make sure, however, you have enough authority in your group to ensure that you will be able to act. This committee will work best if it includes representatives of all the stakeholders—possibly down to the lowest working levels. However, you want to avoid including anyone who is clearly against the initiative. You can bring them in later once you've created sufficient positive momentum.

Example of a how a supportive committee may *not* work

At one time, I was part of a group tasked to plan a major change for an organization. The group had seven members from the company and two outside consultants. We worked intensely four-and-a-half days a week for eight weeks. We came up with a very strong plan, which projected significant yet conservative benefits. The facilities manager who was to enact the plan was part of the committee and seemed to agree with our recommendations.

Our report and presentations were well received, and endorsed by top management. They directed the facilities manager to go ahead with implementation.

Our plan called for using equipment from a particular vendor because we could find no other company with the necessary capabilities.

Unfortunately, the facilities manager had some negative personal history with that company and would not buy from them. He immediately sought alternative sources. As there were no satisfactory alternative vendors, the project ground to a halt. The benefits were never realized.

I don't believe that any of the group members knew beforehand of the manager's antipathy toward the vendor, so I doubt that we could have done anything about it. However, had we known his feelings, it would have been better to excuse him from the group because we recognized early that our success depended on using this vendor.

Task for right now

Now think about which people would be most helpful in launching *your* projected change, the one you envisioned as ***Your Situation*** (page 13). For this first stage, you want a small committee, perhaps five to seven members. Use the principles described above to help you make the selections.

Make a list of possible committee members. And think about who you may *not* want on your committee.

Do this now.

[Your notes]

CREATE YOUR VISION

Developing your Vision is critical! The best Vision is truly *visual*; that is, it can be "seen" in the mind. A list of objectives or goals is good, but people respond best to something they can picture in their mind's eye. It might be about something physical (like a new product) or it might be an achievement (like recognition in an article or on the cover of a journal).

The best Vision statements are those you can expect will endure for a long time—say 10 to 20 years. They provide guidance to the employees, from top to bottom, about how to act in any circumstance. [9]

What will your world look like when you achieve the benefits described in *Your Situation*? Truly imagine how things will be when the changes are fully in place and have become standard operating procedures.

Examples of Vision Statements

Here are four examples of corporate Vision statements; one is a non-profit.

Amazon—We seek to be Earth's most customer-centric company for four primary customer sets: consumers, sellers, enterprises, and content creators. [10]

IKEA—At IKEA our Vision is to create a better everyday life for the many people [sic]. Our business idea supports this Vision by offering a wide range of well-designed, functional home furnishing products at prices so low that as many people as possible will be able to afford them. [11]

PepsiCo—Our Vision is put into action through programs and a focus on environmental stewardship, activities to benefit society, and a commitment to build shareholder value by making PepsiCo a truly sustainable company. [12]

The American Society for the Prevention of Cruelty to Animals (ASPCA) (nonprofit)—"The Vision of the ASPCA is that the United States is a humane community in which all animals are treated with respect and kindness." [13]

Task for right now

Make some notes about this. Take a stab at describing your Vision regarding the change you envision. Do this now.

Remember that your Vision may not be important to others who will be involved. It will show them where you are headed, so you may need additional incentives for others to "buy in."

[Your notes]

USE STRONG COMMUNICATION TOOLS

The *YES I AM Solution*, your carefully-selected committee, and your well-crafted Vision will be of no use unless everyone learns about your Vision and everything else that is happening. Telling people once is not even close to being useful. The project must be in front of everyone at all times. Using all five of Keller and Aiken's benefits (page 27), create at least five different ways to let your people know what is going on. Remember to make your Vision prominent in all that you communicate.

To do this best, use your committee, both to plan and to disseminate your communications. Since the committee represents a range of stakeholders, they are well positioned to help spread the word.

Make sure that all communications go to everyone and will continue for the duration of the project and beyond. See the later section, ***Integrate into the Organization's Culture*** on page 78.

Examples of methods of communication

Kick-off communication example

An electronics company was about to launch a major new venture. [14] The investment was very large even for this company but the potential was equally huge. The leadership needed to have everyone control spending.

A major cost center was their research labs. In general, spending here had been very high because the research payoffs were also great. Even so, the corporate leaders wanted the research people to be extra careful with spending.

A team from the Board of Directors came to the research labs and met with the entire research staff. They fully explained the plans and why they believed in the success. The BoD then asked the staff to control spending as much as possible while not restricting important research work.

Because the research staff members were told the entire story, they felt part of the process. They were able to judge for themselves the merits of the plan and totally supported the BoD's request.

The plan was rolled out; significant funds were preserved in research; and the company successfully entered a lucrative new market.

On-going communications

While a good kick-off is important, the plan and Vision must be in front of everyone continually.

The company can use newsletters, redesigned letterheads with the Vision in its footer, electronic bulletin boards with the Vision in every message, rallies, and reminders at virtually all meetings.

This must continue to be effective. Banners can be used over building entrances. Small group meetings might begin with a review of the progress toward company goals. The Vision is quoted at every opportunity.

Task for right now

Outline the five different motivational messages that will apply for your project. Show how this change will benefit:
- The company
- Society
- Customers
- The working team, and
- Me (the leader or employee), personally.

Define how each of these messages applies to *Your Situation.* Then decide exactly how you can distribute them. Be specific: Call an all-hands meeting, send emails, and create and post announcements. Make notes for these tasks now. Note that you must do all of these and more for it to be useful!

[Your notes]

SEGMENT THE PROJECT

Tackling a project of any substance can be overwhelming for both the Leader and the people. So break it down; create small "bites" each having a well-defined set of activities with a clear goal. Celebrate when each bite has been savored and finished. These bites will create a full meal: your complete project.

What are the parts, the segments, for *Your Situation*, your project? For each part, define or review your SMART goals (p. 53) so that it is clear when you have successfully completed them.

Don't forget these *Chapter 2— Getting Started* activities:

Seek Their Ideas   *their* ideas will enhance yours.

Include Everyone   *they* will surprise you.

Ask for Help   *they* can actually do wonders if given the chance.

Apply the same approaches as you segment your project.

Engage people at all levels. It can be helpful to include your management (supervisors) even up to the top executives. Everyone wants to feel valuable, and getting input from your boss will help your relationship as well as the project. Engaging people above you can be just as important as asking your employees!

Seek ideas as to how to divide up the project. What are the sub-tasks that can be quickly addressed?

Include everyone, and share information as it becomes available.

Then *Ask* them to pick out tasks that they want to lead or where they want to participate. Be prepared to take the risk of allowing your people to have sufficient authority to be successful.

Look at the example, *Engineering Design Quality*, on page 84.

Examples of Segmenting

Remember (Chapter 2 the section on **Your Passion**) when you were considering buying a new inventory system. Assume one of your employees suggested that the team first measure the current stock turns. Ask her to plan the process for this measurement; the completed plan would become the first "bite" on the way to a new inventory system. A second would be executing the measurement and reporting it.

Another bite here might be completing a report that compares available commercial inventory systems to your identified needs.

When you took Sol's place (back at the bottom of page 57) and reached an agreement with the union workers to greatly improve the efficiency for full-scale maintenance, that agreement was an important bite. The workers will have taken another bite from the project when they have completed their first task in a shorter time.

When each task is complete, recognize the employee (or group as appropriate) and celebrate the result.

> **Task for right now**
>
> Again consider *Your Situation*. Make a list of potential bites, segments that can be addressed individually. Consider the specific people who would be suitable to lead or work on each. Then imagine, specifically, the ways they might be helpful.
>
> Remember that you can seek their help in defining the bites and suggesting who might execute these bites.
>
> Take a few moments and make your list now.

[Your notes]

Chapter Five

INSTITUTIONALIZING THE CHANGE

This chapter has two parts: It shows how you can reinforce the progress of your project at significant points; and it tells the importance of making the changes part of your organization's everyday culture.

Relate to the Vision and Continue to Build. Here you connect the value of the project's success to the Vision. This must be done to encourage further work and not allow your people to "slack off." This is particularly important as you approach the conclusion of your original primary objectives. At that time people will begin to think "Oh, we are all done." That can kill your progress.

Integrate into the Organization's Culture. Here you actively find ways to lock the changes into your organization's systems. You build links to daily activities which employees will not want to allow to be changed. This must also be regularly reinforced.

RELATE TO THE VISION AND CONTINUE TO BUILD

As you complete your segments—your *bites*, celebrate them publicly and make clear the relationship of each to your organization's Vision. Recognize the contributions of specific people—as well as whole teams. Show how things are moving forward and what still needs to be done.

Be careful, however, not to claim victory too soon. Your premature claim can actually get people to give up. "Okay, we are there; nothing more needs to be done." President George W. Bush made one of his biggest public mistakes when he prematurely claimed victory in Iraq. [15]

To the contrary, we will realize that as we approach our main objectives there are further places to go. Help the team see that even more benefits are available, and have this keep them moving. Always and repeatedly relate everything to your Vision.

When you have completed many of your bites, take a step backwards and ask what more can be of value?

Examples of *Relate to the Vision and Continuing to Build*

When you are rebuilding your inventory system, you will reach a key objective, a part of your overall goal. You may not be done but it is significant. Of course you will celebrate and as part of that, show how this stage of success supports your overall Vision for your organization.

As you progress on the improvements in your inventory system, you may realize that another system, materials receiving, can be improved as well. Perhaps there are too many returned parts owing to poor quality from a vendor. Point out that we will all gain if we improve this situation (remember **Everyone Benefits**). You might ask them: What do you suggest we do about that?

Task for right now

You can't really act on relating segments to the Vision and continuing to build until you have done many of the earlier pieces, so make a note to remind yourself to return to this section when you're ready to implement this step.

Put a bookmark here, now. Come back to this when the time is right.

[Your notes]

INSTITUTIONALIZING THE CHANGE

INTEGRATE INTO THE ORGANIZATION'S CULTURE

In many ways, integrating your change into the culture is the most important task, and yet it can prove to be the most difficult.

The reason you and your team undertook this entire change project was to gain major benefits or to correct serious problems that existed. Those original difficulties arose from ingrained beliefs and behaviors not easily changed.

You must regularly restate the Vision to reinforce the idea that your team cannot allow people, processes and procedures to return to the old ways. Historically, many organizations have found that when people think that the problem has been solved, they gradually give up the new, successful tools. As a result, many of your benefits will be lost!

Continually point out how recent benefits have been the direct result of the changes; this will help keep people on track. Remind them of how they have been moving toward the Vision and toward their own personal benefits. Show them the connections between the many small successes, the movement toward the Vision, and the benefits for everyone.

Don't let them slip back.

Examples of *Integrating into the Organization's Culture*

Again, look at your change in the inventory system: When it is basically complete point out to your team how their work created this new improved situation. Show that the Vision has been enhanced through their work. Relate the new processes to the organization's growth and show how it has made their lives easier.

Periodically remind the organization how they have improved through the change in the inventory system and how current processes are very effective. That is, reinforce the value of retaining the changes. Do this in various ways and do it often.

As you move to another change—for example the improvement to the materials receiving system—remind everyone about the previous success with the inventory system. Point out that they can do as well here. The success with the changes in the inventory system is evidence that this new change initiative can be a great success too. Work on this second improvement will also reinforce the first set of changes.

Task for right now

Here, as in the previous section, it will be difficult to act on this part until you have actually effected (or at least approached) your change. Remind yourself to return to this section in the future.

Put a bookmark here, now.

[Your notes]

Chapter Six

CHANGE EXAMPLES: FROM GOOD TO AWFUL

You have seen how the key points would work using hypothetical examples. But these tools actually work in the real world! They work remarkably well. And failures can be spectacular when the tools are left in their chests.

In the first section of this chapter on *Successful Changes*, I describe three real cases. The first success is with a very large company that you will know. The second is a smaller company but no less compelling. The third was reported by a former student.

In the next section, *Change So-So's,* I present two cases. The first is an example where the leader initially did not use the change process but later successfully introduced it. The second is one where there are two changes; the first works and the second destroys the first!

The third section, *Failures,* has two examples. The first is a very well known case. The second is a bit different; in it, a very common situation is described which frequently results in change failure.

CHANGE EXAMPLES: FROM GOOD TO AWFUL

SUCCESSFUL CHANGES

For each successful change initiative listed below, I relate the actions to the *YES I AM Solution*.

American Airlines Maintenance Operations (a most amazing example)

In 2004, American Airlines was struggling with financial problems; it decided that it must address the costs of airplane rebuilds.

Every plane goes through an extensive maintenance process to rebuild virtually the entire aircraft. This is done based on a set of rules that includes measures such as hours flown and the number of takeoffs and landings the plane has had. American performed these rebuilds in plants in Oklahoma and, at that time, a rebuild would take about six months of labor and a lot of materials. Rebuilds were very costly!

Carmine Romano, vice president of American's aircraft maintenance facility in Tulsa, was directed to find a way to reduce this cost, particularly that of labor. Now Maintenance Operations was a union shop. Conventional wisdom said the union would never agree to anything which could lead to a possible reduction in membership. In fact, the company had a history of union difficulties. Everyone thought that Romano had no chance of success. In an interview, Wade Goodwyn of National Public Radio (NPR) reported, "At first, Romano was wary of the idea that the only way to avoid bankruptcy was to start *sharing his power* [emphasis added] with his union workers…." He believed that he had no choice; he had to try. [16]

While passionate may not be the right word, perhaps it was more like urgency, clearly Romano really wanted this to succeed. He satisfied the first point: ***Your Passion***.

Romano invited the leaders of the union locals to meet with him. He began by saying that "*we*" have a problem; it was not the company's problem nor was it the union's problem. "*We*" have a problem. If the organization was not able to reduce the rebuild costs, American could fold, and everyone would be out of work.

He told them that we need to cut the rebuild time in half and this has to be done without resorting to overtime. That is, labor costs must be cut in half. He also asked them to accept a significant salary reduction!

I can only imagine the reaction of the union leaders.

He went on to offer them two things: First, he invited the union leaders to become members of the Maintenance Operations management team; they would be part of any business decisions related to this part of the company. Second, there would be no reduction in employees as a result of any reduced work. Not only that, but any reduction in force for any cause (retirement, resignation, etc.) would be replaced: **Everyone Benefits**; he did **Seek Their Ideas** and he acted to **Include Everyone** in the process.

He also told them that the existing union contract will remain in effect. (Of course, they understood that if the company failed, the contract would be worthless.)

Furthermore, he did not bring in engineers from the aircraft manufacturer. He told labor that he believed they knew enough to figure out how to solve the problem. He asked them to do it themselves. He went to them to **Ask for Help**.

I don't know what he did to **Manage Uncertainty**, although I assume that he *and* the union members had a fair amount of anxiety during this process.

I learned about this several years later when I saw a press release from American which announced that Allegiant Air had contracted to have American Airlines Maintenance Services perform their rebuilds. [17] And while the press release came from AA, it quoted Dennis Burchette, Vice President of Transport Workers Union Local 514 in Tulsa. The release reported that Burchette believed this showed the confidence of the industry in the quality of this shop and its union workers. That was interesting!

By the way, as you may already know, corporate press releases almost never quote non-management people. The union-leader's quote was very unusual.

On checking back, I uncovered the story that I just related and learned what had happened. Maintenance had agreed to address the problem and actually reduced costs by 55 percent from the original amount! Rebuilds previously took 20,000 mechanic-days and now take just under 6,000 mechanic-days. As a result, American had many idle skilled workers. They decided to bid for the rebuild work of other airlines. (All airlines must do rebuilds and only the largest have their own shops.) They found that they could win such jobs because their work was high quality *and* their costs were lower than their competition. This, in spite of the fact that American's hourly labor rates were the highest in the industry!

American Airlines turned an expensive money sink into a profit center. Certainly a successful change!

Engineering Design Quality

The following took place at the telecommunications equipment company where I was VP of Engineering.

When a new product was being designed in our company, engineers worked from a Product Requirements document usually provided by Marketing. This describes everything about the product: how it looks, how it works, how it deals with problems—everything. Starting with the Product Requirements document, Engineering first creates a Technical Specification and then develops the product.

To assure that the implementation of a new product design was correct, we had an Engineering Design Assurance (EDA) group. EDA would receive a completed product and test it against the Product Requirements.

I noticed that when a design first reached EDA, it barely took an hour before a problem was detected. When this occurred, the product went back to Engineering for them to make corrections.

Since these first tests related to basic elements of the design—the power supply, for example—fixing the problem often meant modifying many other parts of the design that were affected by the necessary correction. It might have taken several weeks before it could go back to

EDA. I mention the power supply as an example but the first problem may be anywhere.

In this particular case, on returning to EDA, the second testing lasted a few hours before another critical problem was detected. Following standard procedure, the product was returned to Engineering to correct the design. This time the repair took about a week.

The back-and-forth process continued until, finally, both Engineering and EDA were satisfied. The product was then released to Manufacturing.

I decided we needed a better way.

Since we were just starting a new product design, we estimated the likely design time. Experience told us that for a design of this complexity the design would take about 12 weeks. EDA would require another six weeks—18 weeks total. That seemed too long and too expensive. I really wanted this to change.

In previous situations, I had used Concurrent Engineering (CE) [18] as a tool to shorten development and production cycles and thought it would be useful here. In its full form, CE has all elements of product development from concept to customer delivery occurring concurrently.

I decided to try a simplified CE approach on this new design project: Engineering Design and EDA would occur at the same time. Here is how it was to work:

EDA would receive and test a product as soon as anything testable was available—perhaps as little as the circuit board power system, normally an insignificant part of the design. Problems found would be reported to Engineering and corrected. The product would then be retested. As more of the product was completed, testing would be repeated. During the testing process, Engineering would be working on the next stage. When testing went well, Engineering moved on; when a problem arose, Engineering might have to make a few changes in their new work—but very little. At least that was the idea.

Both the design engineers and the EDA engineers thought this was a huge waste of time. The engineers argued that there was no point in

CHANGE EXAMPLES: FROM GOOD TO AWFUL

testing the power system; it was so simple that it was bound to work. Just let us complete the design and then test it. The EDA people said they would just have to retest everything multiple times since the product was not yet done.

I was certain this approach would help us a lot. I was passionate about it. (Remember *Your Passion?*) But how to get them to buy in?

I was the boss, so I could say "just do it," but that seemed counterproductive. They might just work against me; I had been in my position for only four months. So I tried to show them how it would help *them*. I explained what I had observed.

I pointed out that currently, EDA already tested the system multiple times. Often the first problems occurred in the power supply and correcting that usually required redesigning many other parts of the system. If the power system was fixed before other parts were designed, the additional elements would not have to be redesigned to account for the changes in the power system.

If it worked as I described, it would actually be easier for both Engineering and EDA. *(Everyone Benefits.)*

With some misgivings, they agreed to try this approach.

Then I asked them whether there might be some things that could make it work even better than my approach. *(Seek Their Ideas)* One of the best ideas was for EDA to design the test routine at the same time that the circuit was being designed. As it turned out, the test design highlighted points related to product design that Engineering had overlooked. That alone saved significant redesign time! Engineering and EDA agreed to review each other's work—EDA would review the design and Engineering would review the test plan. *(Include Everyone* and *Ask for Help)*

The *Manage Uncertainty* part took no effort here. The working group was a small unit of my organization, and it was easy to know what was going on without formalizing reviews.

The outcome: The overall design time took 13 weeks including the EDA test. This was five weeks shorter than expected—a more than 25-percent saving!

Alan's Story

One day Alan phoned me with a problem. He had taken several courses with me, including one on change management. He hoped that I could help him sort out his problem.

Alan was recently promoted from foreman to supervisor. In his new role, he realized that the company was missing opportunities because they did not have adequate access to operating data from his unit. He wanted to add a data collection and analysis program for his group.

He was certain he knew which program to get. However, as soon as he started to talk about it, some of the group members "pushed back." They did not like this program and did not want it to be installed.

Alan was certain it was the best course of action and was inclined to just do it. He would provide training for the group and thought that it would all work out.

However he remembered the ideas from the class including John Kotter's eight ways to really mess up a change. (See ***Chapter 4—Taking Steps Toward the Goal***). Alan called himself "old school" and was disinclined to try the new ideas. But the new ideas nagged at him, and that was when he phoned me.

We talked about his situation and the relevant change ideas. I did not tell him what to do although we discussed several options.

When I saw Alan again, he was excited to tell me what happened. ***(Your Passion)***

He had accepted the risk and attempted to apply the change tools. He began by asking the lead person for his ideas about how to proceed ***(Seek Their Ideas)***. He invited this person to contribute to the change and buy in. The two discussed the needs and some possible approaches. The man welcomed being asked to help, and he provided several important suggestions.

Alan was more than pleased; he was excited by the man's response. After thinking about their conversation, Alan decided to ask the man to actually run the parts of the change that he had suggested ***(Ask for Help)***. The employee jumped at the chance and got right into it. Not only that,

CHANGE EXAMPLES: FROM GOOD TO AWFUL

the rest of the team became energized by the change in attitude of the lead person *(Include Everyone)* *and* by Alan's leadership.

The program is moving forward and results are even better than Alan could have wished.

Do you see how **YES I AM** worked here?

CHANGE SO-SO'S

Sometimes things take longer than you would like. In the first example below, it took a while for management to realize what needed to be done.

In the second example, one change succeeded and a second failed.

Electronics System Company

Several years ago a large high-technology company decided to expand. Over a one-year period it acquired four separate related companies, each in a different country.

The plan was to integrate corresponding units of each of the companies. The VPs of Engineering were charged with planning and executing the integration of the various engineering groups.

The VPs held a series of meetings during which they discussed the strengths of the several units. This included the technical strengths, areas of current business activity, and the customers and types of contracts held by each. It was clear that some units excelled in mechanical hardware, some in hydraulics, and others in software. Each had the skills in areas needed to deliver on their current contracts.

Because each group had a particular strength, the long-term objective was to combine skills so as to create stronger bids on future contracts.

One of the VPs, Thomas, suggested that they consult with the lower-ranked staff such as department managers. He thought they would have views and knowledge that would be valuable as they planned the integration.

The other VPs did not think it was necessary. They said that they knew their operations very well, and the lower-ranked people would not contribute anything. Not only that, consulting them would take time and delay the overall process.

Thomas did not push his view because he was uncertain himself. Neither he nor any of his peers had any actual experience with mergers or, for that matter, any kind of significant change.

CHANGE EXAMPLES: FROM GOOD TO AWFUL

They decided that since each group had one or more years of current contract work, they could allow things to remain as it was. They were sure that as current work terminated and they began to bid new projects, the various teams would seek to work together. That did not happen.

At the end of two years, the engineering executive team faced the fact that things were not working out as they had hoped. Thomas decided to push his ideas of involving the lower-level managers and personnel.

This lower management group suggested many ideas which the VPs eagerly accepted. Within a few months, cooperation had significantly improved, and new opportunities were being successfully bid.

Thomas accepted that he simply did not know enough to make the change successful at the beginning. The lack of success over the two years drove him to change his stance and become the leader the company needed. [19]

While Thomas cared deeply about the integration of the departments, he was uncertain about the value of his views.

When he realized how important it was to change the approach (*Your Passion*—Thomas'), he put his thoughts out with greater confidence.

When discussing the situation with lower-level managers, he helped them realize how they would benefit from the change. Through the greater integration of the various groups, these managers would have access to the important skills that they needed to make their projects more successful (*Everyone Benefits*).

The managers in turn provided valuable ideas which were accepted. (*Seek Their Ideas* and *Include Everyone*)

In this case, it was clear that the managers would act on the new ideas. (*Ask for Help*)

I don't know how Thomas handled *Manage Uncertainty*.

Medical Services Company

In 2006 there was a division of a medical services company in Florida which was not doing very well. The patient-to-professional ratio, a measure of a company's strength, was the lowest of the thirteen company divisions in the state. At that time, the company hired a person to be both part of the staff and also to run this division. In the manager role, he was specifically charged with expanding the number of patients. [20]

He created a marketing plan to increase the number of patients seen. To do this he worked closely with the other people in the division, both the professionals and the support staff. He sought their ideas and used most of them. He viewed the people in the division as a family. His passion, marketing program and involvement of the people were so successful that in two years his organization became the top performing division in the state! From the bottom to the top in two years!

About that time the whole company (it was a multi-state operation) was bought by another firm in the field. One of the first actions by the new owners was to discontinue the marketing program in the division discussed here. The manager and staff tried to convince the owners of the value of marketing to no avail.

Almost immediately the patient load in the company began to decrease. The professional staff continued to try to get management to resume the marketing program but they got nowhere.

In frustration, a number of staff members left the company.

In 2014, this division of the medical services company was closed down!

What happened?

When the new division manager was hired, the original owners encouraged him to use his ideas to build the division. He welcomed the freedom and became passionate about the division's success (Remember

CHANGE EXAMPLES: FROM GOOD TO AWFUL

Your Passion?). He listened to the employees and cared about their suggestions (***Seek Their Ideas***). As a result, the company's ***Employees Benefited*** from the improvement in business. The division manager acted to ***Include Everyone.*** The overall effect of the changes was to make the business the strongest division in the state!

After the sale of the company, however, the new corporate management seemed to ignore the employees and rejected any ideas. The regional manager specifically cancelled the marketing efforts which had been so successful. This manager rejected feedback from the division and eventually employees stopped trying to help.

When the employees were engaged in the life of the division, the company flourished; when the employees were ignored, the division died!

The new owners had no interest in any of the well-known modern approaches to management, not to mention change, and lost out.

FAILURES

Sometimes the attempt is a total loss; sometimes benefits simply aren't realized. Our first example focuses on the well-known—and very unfortunate—**AOL/Time-Warner** merger. The second case reports the experience of a salesperson whose customers would struggle with change.

AOL/Time-Warner

This was a merger made in heaven—or so thought each company's management. Time-Warner was a company that created content, and AOL was a communications company that distributed content. This seemed like a natural fit.

In the year 2000, both were doing reasonably well. On the communications side, AOL had 20 million subscribers, and Time-Warner had 13 million. The combination would become the nation's largest online provider. [21] With the expected continued growth of the Internet and all types of communications services, this expanded customer base was going to blossom. The merged company would eat up the competition.

What's more, Time-Warner brought to the table a wide range of media sources including Warner Bros. Studios, HBO, CNN, Warner Music, and Time magazine, as well as some new Internet media companies. Content was being called "King," and this company had it—in spades! Information, entertainment, music, books, movies, video—they had it all!

How could it not be a huge success?

But right from the beginning, there seemed to be no effort made to integrate their operations. [22] In 2002, the joint company had a loss of $99 billion; its stock had dropped 70 percent since the merger.

It took until 2009 to create a de-merger agreement. [23] They separated with the value of the two companies substantially less than when they merged!

The whys are laid out by Larry Kramer in an article in *The Daily Beast*. [24] It was clear that the men at the top were passionate about the merger. Steve Case at AOL and Gerald Levin at Time-Warner both

CHANGE EXAMPLES: FROM GOOD TO AWFUL

pushed this deal. They argued the points above. They got *"Your Passion"* in the *YES I AM* model.

It became apparent that there were problems with both information and process. On the information side, it appears that AOL had inflated its revenue figures. But even so, that was not a stopper. As for process, they didn't seem to have any organized approach to making the change work.

Kramer reported that the Time-Warner management, below Levin, did not like or value AOL; they thought the merger was a waste of time and money. Few people were actually participating, so few had a stake in the success. There was no effort from the top to try to get people to help make this work. Actually, many at T-W feared that AOL would try to take over the whole operation, so they would not work with the AOL people.

Everyone Benefits? Upper management didn't even try to show the employee benefits, and, clearly, people did not see benefits for themselves.

In fact, most were certain: They could not imagine any possible benefits for themselves.

After that, **Seek Their Ideas**, **Include Everyone** and **Ask for Help** were never going to happen. We don't know what they might have done regarding **Manage Uncertainty**.

Except for the top executives, no one seemed to care about the success of the merger.

While they had *Your Passion*, the rest of the steps for successful change were never tried.

It seems as though this deal was in trouble before it even started—but it took the merged companies many years to bury the merger!

An ERM System

I was speaking with a man who sells Enterprise Resource Management (ERM) systems for a major manufacturer. [25] I told him my thoughts on the low rate of successful change and suggested that he probably did not see this problem in his work. After all, he sold one of the premiere product lines in the field.

Not so! he told me. System installations frequently fail to provide the desired benefits for the customer.

I was amazed!

"Why?" I asked.

He said that customers usually requested a system installation based on the vendor's standard setup. But the standard setup is rarely best for any given customer. Once the standard setup is selected, the vendor's sales rep is kept from digging down into the customer's needs and adjusting the system to satisfy them. Customers are frequently certain that the standard installation will meet their needs, and they decline further help.

As a result, this expensive, complicated, software system worked—but it failed to provide the benefits expected.

Clearly business leaders really want these new systems. Perhaps they are even passionate about them. We will give them *Your Passion* but they never get to *E, S, I, A,* or *M!*

These leaders don't seem to consider how *Everyone Benefits*.

Neither do they go to their employees to *Seek Their Ideas* or *Include Employees* in the change process (except to tell them what to do), or *Ask for Help*. One major issue: There often are needed capabilities known only to the employees, but no one asks them.

These leaders *Manage Uncertainty* by keeping everything under their control!

They are like the Confident Leader whom we will meet in Chapter 7. They are so certain they know what must be done that they underestimate the complexity of the relationship between an ERM system and company operations. They see it as a simple purchase like Word® or Excel®, which, by the way, are significant changes also! Therefore, they may not even realize that implementing ERM constitutes a change which must be managed to be effective.

Chapter Seven

CHANGE FAILED? NOT YOURS!

Now, the *YES I AM Solution* works—when it is used. The tools in many of the other books on change also work *when used*. Thirty percent of change initiatives do work! So why the high failure rate!

The only logical conclusion is that leaders frequently don't use these tools. But why? What is it that blocks leaders from success?

Let's remember the process:

Start with the employees. Remember that all of the tools address the concerns of the employees. They focus on getting the workers to do the right things.

In the face of a change initiative, when a company is introducing something new, people may worry about their ability to do what will be asked of them. Perhaps there will be a new technology which may be difficult to learn. They may be asked to work longer hours than they would like. Perhaps the employees will get a new boss; and they will wonder whether they will still be valued. They may be concerned that their jobs are threatened. They may become very anxious.

Often they spend a lot of time with these concerns. As a result, they fret and talk with their co-workers: What are the current rumors? Has anyone left or been laid off? Who will their new leader be? Will their division be merged with another, or even dissolved?

Frequently employees know a lot about the current difficulties that the organization is facing. Involving these employees would provide an opportunity to improve the change plan and get an even better result than originally sought. (I discussed this in the earlier chapters.)

So the authors of change management books have provided an array of tools that can be used to allay employee concerns and engage them in the change process. You can probably think of many ways yourself. You know it is important to get your employees to want to help you make the change a success. That is what these tools will help you do.

Look at the basic set of tools I've provided in this book: the ***YES I AM Solution***. Notice that after the Y, the next four work by *giving power to the employees.*

Give power to employees? Uh-oh!

When leading a change initiative, two words can get a leader into difficulty: **Uncertainty** and **Certainty.** There are dangers in both.

When facing a new situation, you may have a high degree of *uncertainty*. You may need help, but feel *uncertain* as to how to get it. You may be afraid to ask for help as that would reveal your lack of confidence. Thus you will move ahead without adequate knowledge.

On the other hand, when you know a great deal about a situation and are sure you know how to approach it, you have a high degree of certainty and confidence as to what must be done. This can lead you to believe that you don't need any help.

Either of these polar opposites can cause leaders to ignore the very tools which could help them. Both extremes will get leaders into trouble.

In either case, ***the leader is unlikely to give power to employees!***

Back in ***Chapter 1—Introduction*** (page 7), I introduced a list of seven situations in which leaders fail to use the available tools. Now we'll look at how each of these leaders limits their success. For each leader, I'll provide an example of the problem, a discussion of the cause, and some ideas about fixing it.

I have provided a short instrument which will help you explore *your* style in using change. It is called ***What Kind of Change Leader Are You?*** You will find it in ***Appendix B.***

Let's dig deeper, beginning with anxiety.

THE ANXIOUS LEADER

> The anxious leader (like the employees) is apprehensive about the success of the proposed changes, and therefore feels a need to tightly control the change process.

Frequently, change initiators—the leaders—have doubts about the success of the initiative. They may have thoughts such as: Will I succeed with this important change? Do I know enough to make it all work? How can I ensure a good outcome? What will happen to me if I don't succeed?

Leaders are human and have the same concerns and worries as any employee.

What do people do when they are worried? Many try to maintain control (in the traditional sense). In these cases, it means making sure that everyone *does things right*: "I better tell them what to do, and I better make sure that they do it!"

We have seen that when you use the change tools, you will be *giving* power to employees! Wait a minute—suppose that *you* are anxious! *You* must make sure that things get done correctly. *You* must maintain control. *You* have to tell each employee what to do. Give them power? Not very likely!

But our premise is that the way to succeed is to use the tools, the tools which give the employees power. You cannot have it both ways. But you are thinking, "What about my control? I'm supposed to know what to do."

Meet Laura, an Anxious Leader

When Laura needs to introduce changes in a field where she feels weak, she will be anxious and uncomfortable with her lack of knowledge. She is unlikely to involve any lower-level employees because she believes that she must totally control the situation; it is the only way she will feel safe. To **Seek Their Ideas** means both exposing her lack of knowledge and giving control to others. The first is embarrassing, and the second requires risking the project on the performance of others.

While Laura is laying out the steps, she will worry that she may be wrong, owing to her lack of knowledge. She will also be concerned about giving assignments to people who may not be the best for the tasks. Thus she will spell out the details and the time-line for each step. She will keep track of the work and expect everything will be completed at the times she specified. She will also monitor the work closely—micromanaging it!

Look at what she loses:

By not asking for ideas, she loses the opportunity to improve her plan and make better choices as to which person is to implement each part of the change. She also loses the opportunity to show that her employees are important to her, leaving them with little interest in doing the best possible job. And they will have greater concerns about their security. In summary, she:
- Missed good ideas,
- Missed employees feeling valued,
- Missed employees feeling committed to the success of the project, and thus
- Missed getting the needed benefits!

Do you want to be her?

Some Help for the Anxious Leader

Have you noticed that you have strong concerns about a change you are trying to initiate? Look at **Your Situation**—yes the one you identified at the beginning of Chapter 2 (page 20)—and start by making a list of these concerns.

Now step back and see how you can apply the **YES I AM Solution**. Take it step by step; review each point and see how it might be used in **Your Situation**

Where is **Your Passion?** Unless you are passionate, you won't have the strength to take the necessary risks.

Next look for how **Everyone Benefits.** Help your employees see that it is in their best interest. Do it now! Work with them to make sure they really understand how they will be better off with the new situation. Even better, let *them* help figure out how they would benefit.

Now **Seek Their Ideas** for making the plan *very* much better. Find out what issues have not been addressed. Are there ongoing concerns you and your staff hope to address as part of this initiative? Take everyone's ideas and improve your approach—and be sure you let them know that you *value* their contributions.

As things progress **Include Employees** whenever possible by giving them information updates (such as in meetings and with memos). Show them that they are important to your organization. It may take some time to convince them; however, the improved motivation will eventually pay for itself.

Next go back to them and directly **Ask for Help**. Ask them to select the tasks which they would like to do and think that they could do well.

You may have difficulty letting go of control. However, even if loss of control is not your issue, you will do well to use monitoring activities. Monitoring helps **Manage Uncertainty**. Set up review meetings, emergency situation reports, and anything else which will help you feel confident.

Here too, get their ideas. They may suggest better ways for you to remain comfortable as the project goes forward.

[Your notes]

THE CONFIDENT LEADER

> These leaders are so confident of their own knowledge, skills and resources, they feel no need to ask for help from their employees.

Sometimes, the change initiators are personally very confident about the success of the initiative as in the ERM situation in the **Failures** section of Chapter 6. These initiators know the field very well and are sure of the steps needed for the change. They have no concerns about what has to be done; they have been there before and "it's a piece of cake."

They have also read the books and know all about change, so they think they know how to lay out the steps and assign the tasks. It will all go fine.

So where is the Achilles heel?

To begin, it's highly unlikely that leaders know *everything* about the situation. Remember that their employees are doing the work day-by-day and may know things the leaders don't.

What's more, even if these leaders truly know what is necessary, the employees must still carry out the work. For the best result, the leaders must get those employees to really want the project to succeed.

Many writers say "Give power to employees!" But since these leaders know the situation really well, they think, "Why bother?"

Here is an example of how this situation might look.

Meet Anne, a Confident Leader

Since the necessary changes are in a field that Anne knows and understands well, she will likely plan the change herself—or perhaps with a consultant or two. She is unlikely to engage any lower-level employees—why bother? She knows enough to do it well all by herself.

She will lay out the steps and assign the tasks. She will specify the details of each step along her self-designed timeline. She will keep track of the work and expect all of it to be completed at the times she ordered.

Look at what she loses:

By not asking for ideas, she loses the opportunity to make her plan even better. Also, her employees will get the message that they are not important. That leads the employees to have greater concerns about their security. As a result, they will have little interest in doing the best possible job. In summary, she:
- Missed good ideas,
- Missed employees feeling valued,
- Missed employees feeling committed to the success of the project, and thus
- Missed getting the needed benefits!

Wait a minute! This is the same set of losses as in the first situation. Do you want to be Anne?

> **Some Help for the Confident Leader**
>
> Perhaps you are very knowledgeable about the details of the change you wish to introduce, not to mention understanding the process to introduce the required change. However a motivated team will be more productive, resulting in a shorter time to your objective. Thus you may still benefit greatly from the *YES I AM Solution.* Here is how you might proceed:
>
> *Your Passion* is clear; you really want this to happen. So look at how *Everyone Benefits.* Help your employees see that it is in their interests to make this a success. Then move on with the model. Here are three steps to take.
>
> First, there are likely to be some problems which employees would be first to catch. *Seek Their Ideas* and help make an already good plan better.

Second, if there are no problems, simply involving and listening to your employees will give them the message that they are truly valued. *(Involve Everyone)*

Third, if none of their ideas are useful, ***Ask for Help*** anyway. You may be surprised by their choices. By having the employees select the tasks they want to do, you will increase their incentive to do them well.

In all three cases, the employees feel inspired and motivated to want to perform better.

You may feel confident that you can do it yourself and perhaps you can. After all, using the ***YES I AM Solution*** may introduce uncertainty and make you uncomfortable. Thus you need to do something to ***Manage Uncertainty***. As I have said, what works for me are regular meetings and an employee's promise to alert me immediately when problems arise. You may have to find another—your own—method.

Take it step by step; see if you are willing to take the risks, letting go of control. This may be uncomfortable but look at what you can gain. Go back over the points and see how each might be used in ***Your Situation***—yes the one you identified at the beginning of Chapter 2 (page 20)

[Your notes]

THE HURRIED LEADER

> The hurried leader decides that the change is so urgent that there is not enough time to use these tools.

Projects are often tightly constrained by time. Hurried leaders worry that there simply won't be enough time to complete all the necessary tasks. They have read the books and have decided that following the usual instructions for successful change will take a lot of time—time they simply don't have.

They decide to move ahead as best they know how. Such a leader may think, "I'll fix any problems that occur, and we'll get done faster."

Meet Joleen, the Hurried Leader

Joleen believes there is barely enough time to execute the change—the pressure is on.

A big convention is coming up, and the new product must be ready. She is convinced that there simply is not enough time. She worries that if she doesn't act fast, the project will fail and her career along with it!

She can easily say that she meets the first requirement: **Your Passion**. She cares deeply about the product's success, but she can't spare the time to convince her employees that **Everyone Benefits**.

To **Seek Their Ideas** would require even more time; this can't be done. And so it goes with each of the remaining change tools.

Look at what she loses:

She loses all of the same elements lost by the Anxious and Confident Leaders.

Ironically she also risks losing time! She had shied away from these activities because they would take too long. Remember the old saw? We didn't have time to do it right but we had time to do it over!

Failing to excite her employees forfeits the very energy which could speed the project. While getting started may be slow, the project will move quickly once it is underway.

The missed ideas and the lack of employee interest jeopardize the project's success and may cause the very delays which have worried her from the beginning.

> **Some Help for the Hurried Leader**
>
> You might identify with this leader—you simply don't have enough time. *The YES I AM* **Solution** will take time you just don't have. *Your Passion* may not be enough to get you through.
>
> But look what can happen if you show them the urgency of the task and seek their help using the model. You will engage them. You will motivate them to want to make the project a success.
>
> You may not be comfortable asking for help from your employees. This might seem very risky, when actually it can be of great value. Together you can see how ***Everyone Benefits***; you can ***Seek Their Ideas*** to make the project work better and flow faster; when you ***Include Everyone*** and ***Ask for Help*** you will see how much faster things will progress.
>
> Every part of the model can help speed things along. Look at the opening story of this book ***The change that challenged me to lead…*** That had a critical time line. Go to ***Epilogue & Summary*** which revisits the opening story and tells how it came out.

When time is tight, engaged, motivated support can actually improve the chances for the success of a risky endeavor. It may feel slow initially, but the group's new energy can recover the lost time. And this applies even when the change process is well along.

[Your notes]

THE "EDUCATED" LEADER

> The "educated" leader can tell you exactly what must be done in the change process; however, this leader does not actually know how to use the tools in the real world.

These leaders have studied the books, taken the classes, and attended the online seminars. They can tell you exactly what must be done and the value each step provides. They know that it is important to empower employees and why that is valuable. They know that employees grow with recognition of their work. These leaders have also read that their people have a lot of knowledge.

But when it comes to acting—actually seeking their ideas, including them in planning, asking for their help—these leaders do not know where to start.

Meet Art, the "Educated" Leader

Art's project is important. The benefits to his organization will be great. Art knows that the employees are very concerned about the project and how it will impact them.

He has been a good student and has read many books on change management. His approach is to *tell* everyone how important the change is. He *describes* the Vision and *explains* why having a good clear Vision is important.

Here is how Art might work: He may form a project steering committee and guide it to arrive at *his* ideas. He might say to an employee "Here is what I think you should do. Are you okay with that?"

He even tells his employees that he is empowering them and that he hopes that doing so will make them want to make the change a success. He might say "I know that you will be successful with your assigned task because you have great skills."

Look at what he loses:

He loses the same things as the Anxious and Hurried Leaders: better plans, commitment, and success!

Art fails to get much help from his people. He is puzzled by the lack of support which he expected. After all, he believes that he has been doing all of the right things. Yet everything continues to go slowly—or not at all.

Some Help for the Educated Leader

If you think you may be an Educated Leader like Art, think about your plan and ask yourself, "What must be done here? *Exactly* what must be done here? What are the component steps? What might be useful intermediate goals? What must I do first thing tomorrow morning?" Be very specific with your answers. If you find these questions difficult, keep reading.

When you view **Your Situation**, I assume that you will find Y**ou are Passionate** about the desired objectives so let's move on.

When you look at how **Everyone Benefits,** you might tell the employees that "the change will be good for you because the company will be doing better." Some leaders do not understand that the employees won't see the situation that way. How about asking them where *they* see the benefits for themselves? Or what benefits would they like to get? **Seek Their Ideas** for their benefits. As an example, point out that a successful project will increase company profits and some of that might be used for community improvements

This approach also addresses the empowering case: By regularly providing opportunities for the employees to ask about the project *(Include Everyone)*, the leader is actually empowering them! Now there is no need to say anything about empowering. Then you might *Ask for Help*; let them suggest how they can help.

As you do each of these activities, pay particular attention to how your actions may be different from what you would normally do. Also try to observe how you *feel* as you do each task—not what you think but how you feel. And finally, see if you can put yourself in the place of one of your employees; how would that person feel?

When you see how this works for you, go back to *Chapter 2—Getting Started—The YES I AM Solution* and review the other parts of the model. Think about how each can apply in *Your Situation* and try it out.

This will help you learn to better implement your knowledge.

[Your notes]

THE MISTRUSTFUL LEADER

The mistrustful leader lacks faith in the techniques and distrusts the employees.

These leaders may have had many years of experience and know how necessary it is to be very clear with employees. These leaders believe that employees come to work to earn a living without caring very much about the work. Employees must be told what to do, and leaders must keep after them to be certain that the work is done, and done as directed.

Meet Matt, the Mistrustful Leader

Suppose that Matt's production area needs a new piece of equipment. He calls in the shop foreman, Joe, and explains what must happen:

"I want you to tell Sam to clear the 200-square-foot area just inside the entrance to make room for the machine. Give him four days to get it done.

"Then tell Amanda to write the modified directions for our specific installation. She can have two days to do that."

Joe interrupts him to say, "Wait a minute; I have an idea. What if we see which area of the shop is the least used. I am not sure it is the area near the entrance."

Matt tells him, "Don't worry about it; just do it.

"I'm going to stop by tomorrow to check in. I hope this works out well."

See if you can imagine how Joe, Sam, and Amanda feel. How would *you* feel if you were any one of them? And, by the way, how do you think Matt feels?

Some Help for the Mistrustful Leader

Do you resonate with Matt's approach? If so, you are not alone. And you may be correct in your actions—at least sometimes. Even so, you may find some things here that you can use.

Mistrustful Leaders have had experiences that convinced them that workers cannot be counted on to deliver. These leaders are certain that giving freedom to employees will only result in work not getting done.

Perhaps these leaders have not given their employees a chance to show what they can do. Maybe, like the Uninformed Leader discussed next, they don't know how to manage any other way. For many such leaders, even considering seeking employees' help can create anxiety. (Perhaps not unlike the Anxious Leader described earlier.)

Do you think you could try just one of the elements of the **YES I AM Solution?** Perhaps you could ask your employees what they think may be a **Benefit** for them—or ask just one employee.

Or you could try this: Go back and reread the section, **Ask for Help** on p. 42. Read it as if you were the employee. Pay particular attention to how you feel—not how you think—as you experience the situation.

The Mistrustful Leader may be more comfortable beginning with small steps. Focus on one tool at a time with just one person. See how it works and how you feel as you use it. Then try another tool, or the same tool with other people.

You also might read the next section on the Uninformed Leader. It gives other views of Matt's situation with Jan and Jean.

[Your notes]

THE UNINFORMED LEADER

> The uninformed leader simply has no knowledge of how change processes work.

These leaders often act much like Mistrustful Leaders, but their behavior comes from not knowing they have alternatives. They have not studied or read about introducing change. If they have experienced a change situation, it is likely to have been poorly handled. So they know little and will only do whatever seems useful.

Some leaders have excellent instincts in these areas and may, without formal knowledge, actually do the right things. These exceptional people care about their employees and may be able to trust them; they instinctively want to work together with their employees. It simply seems natural to them. Such leaders have instincts which place them among the 30 percent of successful initiatives. They may never actually realize just how remarkable they are!

But many Uninformed Leaders just do not understand how to help people be as effective as they could be. Even when employees want to help, these leaders do not realize the potential benefits.

Meet Jean and Jan, two types of Uninformed Leaders

Neither of these leaders are familiar with the tools for change; they have not read any of the books nor taken any courses. Jean simply doesn't know what can be useful when introducing change while Jan has naturally good instincts.

Let's begin with Jean.

As in the Mistrustful Leader's case, Jean's production area needs a new piece of equipment. She calls in the shop foreman, Mike, and explains what is to happen.

> "I want you to tell Sam to clear the 200 square foot area just inside the entrance to make room for the machine. Give him four days to get it done.

> "Then tell Amanda to write the modified directions for our specific installation. She can have two days to do that."
>
> Mike interrupts her to say, "Wait a minute; I have an idea. What if we see which area of the shop is the least used. I am not sure it is the area near the entrance."
>
> Jean is unsure of the value of Mike's suggestion, but she is quite sure she knows what to do.
>
> Jean says, "I think the entrance will be okay. Just go on and have Amanda work out how to do the installation.
>
> "I'll stop by tomorrow to check in."

See if you can imagine how Mike, Sam, and Amanda are feeling. How do you think Jean is feeling?

Summary: Jean has the possibility of growing if she is willing to take a risk by learning and trying tools for effective change management.

Now let's see what Jan might do.

She starts off the same as Jean but see what happens when Mike interrupts her to say,

> "Wait a minute; I have an idea. What if we see which area of the shop is the least used. I am not sure it is the area near the entrance."
>
> Jan is unsure of the value of Mike's suggestion, but she is willing to consider it. She is interested in what Mike has to say, and with that the whole situation becomes different.
>
> Jan says, "Why don't you follow up on your idea, and see where we might place the equipment. I'll stop by tomorrow, and we will see what you have learned."

Again, see if you can imagine how Mike, Sam, and Amanda will be feeling in this case—and how Jan is feeling.

Summary: Jan intuitively makes good leadership choices; by studying the change management tools, she has the possibility of becoming even more successful!

> **Some Help for the Uninformed Leader**
>
> If you identify with either of these leaders, you have a good opportunity to become successful. You won't have to unlearn many non-productive behaviors. If you are like Jan, reading this book will help you see why you have been effective and help you do even better. If you are like Jean, reading this book will open your eyes to new ways to introduce change. In either case, if you did not work through all of the sample tasks, now would be a good time to do it.
>
> Go to *Your Situation* and start using the points in the *YES I AM Solution.* Think about what you want to accomplish and see what *Your Passion* looks like. Then go on to the other five points and see where they get you.
>
> But you can go even further if you take advantage of the many other fine books and programs available. I have already mentioned some, and the Internet will yield a wealth of material.
>
> In addition, you can find professional organizations that provide specific training for growing effective leaders. *You* can be a successful leader.

[Your notes]

THE WRONG-CHANGE LEADER

> The wrong-change leader has introduced a change all right—but it's the wrong one!

These leaders decide that certain improvements are necessary and identify some options. They make decisions and act on them.

Their actions do not solve anything because the leaders usually don't fully understand the problems in the first place."

Meet Dante, the Wrong-Change Leader

We find Dante at an industry convention, wandering among the vendors. An exhibit catches his eye.

The vendor is talking about a situation that sounds just like something in Dante's office. The representative's presentation seems to cover exactly what is happening at home!

Dante listens and asks some questions. He is getting more excited by the minute. He thinks this is *exactly* what they need in his company! The price is high, but it would be very reasonable if it solves the problem.

He places an order on the spot!

Once purchased, delivered and installed, the product simply fails to solve the problem. It turns out there was much more to the situation than Dante knew. As a result, it was the *wrong change* to introduce.

Again, by not using the tools, the change he introduced could not deliver the necessary desired results.

Some Help for the Wrong-Change Leader

You can find yourself like this leader if you discover that you have been implementing the wrong change. You have chosen the wrong approach for the goals you are seeking or possibly it is the goal itself which is wrong. In most cases, all is not lost. At this point, you can stop the current process and apply some of the change tools. Doing so can prove productive—if it demonstrates the leader's willingness to work with the employees.

A good start might be to tell your group that you need to change what you are doing. Be honest about it. Tell them why the goals or methods will not work.

Go to the beginning of the *YES I AM Solution* and share *Your Passion* and the urgency of the objectives. Help them see how what you want to do now will benefit them *(Everyone Benefits)*. You *Seek Ideas* to be sure you get it right this time; ask them what was missing, what needs to be done, what is getting in the way, and more.

Then continue with the *YES I AM Solution* and off you go!

Remember the story in *Chapter 6—Electronics Systems Company,* where the leader was on an unproductive path for over two years before he realized that something different must be done. Two years! When he finally engaged the lower level managers, they moved forward—and fast.

[Your notes]

EPILOGUE & SUMMARY

THE CHANGE THAT CHALLENGED ME TO LEAD… (CONT.)

Back in the Prologue, I left off where I was feeling stuck and worried. I told you that this gave me the basis for my **YES I AM Solution.**

Now here is how the optical fiber communications project came out.

One day, as I approached the coffee urn where the men gathered for breaks, I noticed that their conversation had changed. Normally, I would hear them discussing something like last night's Yankees game—we were in the New York area after all! But today they were talking about the project: *How might we do this? What do we need to learn? Where can we get advice?*

Whoa! They were already working on the project in their heads. I began to think maybe things *were* going to work out after all!

Mel's request

Several weeks along, Mel, my most experienced engineer, dropped into my office shortly before our team meeting.

We started chatting, but I realized he had something on his mind. I let the conversation go on for a while and then said: "Something's on your mind, Mel. Spit it out."

After some hemming and hawing, he said, "I think I should lead the project."

I said, "Of course! I agree. Why don't you tell that to the group at the meeting today?"

"Well, I don't know…"

EPILOGUE & SUMMARY

As usual, the meeting began with reviewing and revising our task lists. This went on for the better part of an hour while I hoped Mel would say something. No such luck!

I finally said, "Just before our meeting Mel came to my office. He told me that he thought he should be the project lead."

John turned to Mel, "Did you say that?"

"Yes," said Mel.

"Did you mean it? Do you want to lead the project?"

"Sure!"

"Will you let Mel lead?" John asked me.

"Of course; he is the right person to do it."

"In that case," said John as he pointed toward our task list, "I would like to design the photo-detector."

Immediately, other engineers started to claim tasks on the list. In less than ten minutes every essential task was claimed!

Then Matt said, "May I also do one of the other tasks? The one I have seems rather small."

"Of course." And soon the team picked up several other secondary tasks.

It was almost four weeks into the schedule, but we were off and seriously running!

Follow up meetings

After that we met every two weeks to check in. I spent very little time with the members of the team except when someone wanted my thoughts on an issue.

Several engineers in the company's semiconductor division had been involved in these meetings and their contributions were built into the project.

I was amazed how well everyone cooperated. Questions would arise and they would seek help from each other or from people elsewhere in the company. I felt very secure in the project.

Between Mel leading the team and everyone wanting the project to succeed, I had little to do!

Five months later

Phil, my department head, and several of his peers joined me to walk from lab to lab and see the results. Every engineer exceeded the objectives of his task! Even the secondary tasks which had been addressed succeeded. The project was an overwhelming success!

And with that, the company decided that optical fiber was the future of undersea communications. [26]

Today undersea optical fiber communications is ubiquitous—all arising from that project!

EPILOGUE & SUMMARY

THE BASIC MODEL REVISITED

So there you have it.

The company needed to know if optical fibers could be used for undersea systems. My project began with an urgent need just as described in the *Getting Started* chapter in the beginning of the *Your Passion* section. Then...

Your Passion—This was about me: I surely was passionate about this project.

Everyone Benefits—Everyone in the team realized that this was a great opportunity to get a "kick-start" into an exciting new technology.

Seek Their Ideas—I asked them to help decide how to create the project and what elements it needed to have. They jumped at the chance and together we designed the entire system architecture.

Include Everyone—Many people were involved from the beginning including those from other groups. Ultimately, they self-selected, and those most suitable to contribute to the project dug in. The result was a very strong team.

Ask for Help—Once the architecture was set, I could have assigned the elements to the engineers. However, they were so engaged in the planning that I gave them the chance to choose their own tasks, and they loved it.

Manage Uncertainty—As I watched and worried, the team began to show me at the coffee urn that they were going to make this work. I added some meetings and made certain that I would be told of difficulties, and my uncertainty was under control!

My own fear was strongest in the earliest stages when I could not tell what was going to happen. But I acted *as if* I trusted the team, and they didn't let me down.

They knew that this was important and that I was asking for their help. I was showing that I valued them. By me giving up control, they wanted to show that they could do it. I had more power because I gave it away. They would have done anything I asked!

Remember *Your Situation*

Now let's return to **Your Situation,** the one you thought about back in **Chapter 2—Getting Started—The YES I AM Solution**. What is that specific objective you want to achieve where others will be affected by your actions? (p. 20)

Review the notes you made as you learned about the **YES I AM** points. See how you can improve them now.

Now it's your turn to create your own success case.

You will have to take risks, but **"M"** (**Manage Uncertainty**) is there to help you handle them. Leaders must take risks, or they get nowhere.

This book contains a lot

This short book is intended to help you make your change initiative successful. I hope it challenges you not only to consider your employees' capabilities, but also to examine your normal approach to change.

Then as you regard each of the six *YES I AM* points, think about how you might use each one. Don't commit to doing anything yet, but plan how you would use each. Look closely at how you are reacting to each idea. Does it feel good? Does it feel awkward? What other feelings are you having? You need to be aware of all of this, so you can help yourself address those issues.

Trying to do it all at once may be too much. Each of the tools from *YES I AM* to *Institutionalizing the Change* can be applied individually. Begin with what feels comfortable.

Note that using this material will itself be a change in the way you work. You might consider applying the book's tools to the process of adding change tools to your leadership style.

A key idea in using the material here is to do it with *awareness*. That is, pay attention to what is happening as you use the *YES I AM Solution*

EPILOGUE & SUMMARY

and the other ideas in this book. If I had been consciously aware of the change management tools earlier in my career, I believe I would have been an even more effective leader.

You can do things just like you always have and get the same results—or you can take a chance on the ideas presented here. Then you can

Lead Change Without Fear

by using

The YES I AM Solution

LIST OF APPENDICES

Appendix A: Expanded Table of Contents   131
Appendix B: What kind of Change Leader are you?   135
Appendix C: Types of change and how they appear   139
Appendix D: Short history of change   141

APPENDIX A

EXPANDED TABLE OF CONTENTS

Dedication ·· iii
Acknowledgements ··· v
Prologue & Preface ·· 1
   The change that challenged me to lead… ··························· 1
      The next day ·· 2
      Skill sets: Analog vs. fiber/laser ································· 2
      Participative management ·· 3
      Fear and anxiety—mine ·· 4
   Why I wrote this book ··· 5
Chapter One—Introduction ··· 7
      How change is introduced ·· 8
      The effect of change on employees ···························· 8
      The leader's role and difficulties ······························ 9
   Approaches to Change ··· 10
   My Approach and Solution ··· 12
      Outline of this book ·· 13
      How to get the most out of this book ······················ 15
Chapter Two—Getting Started—The YES I AM Solution ········ 19
      Your Situation ·· 20
   Your Passion ·· 22
      How do passion and urgency drive the change process? ·· 23
      What we have done so far in YES I AM: ··················· 24
      Task for right now ·· 24
   Everyone Benefits ··· 26
      What's in it for me? ·· 26
      Example of how you might approach Everyone Benefits: · 28

EXPANDED TABLE OF CONTENTS

    What we have done so far in YES I AM: 29
    Task for right now 29
  Seek Their Ideas 31
    Example of how you might approach Seek Their Ideas .. 32
    What we have done so far in YES I AM: 34
    Task for right now 35
  Include Everyone 37
    Examples of how you might Include Everyone 37
    What we have done so far in YES I AM: 39
    Task for right now 40
  Ask for Help 42
    Example of how you might Ask for Help 42
    Asking for help 44
    What we have done so far in YES I AM: 44
    Task for right now 45
  Manage Uncertainty 48
    Example of how to Manage Uncertainty 48
    We have completed all elements in YES I AM: 49
    Task for right now 50

Chapter Three—The Role of Control **53**
    Example of Traditional Control Methods 54
    Analysis 55
    Example of the YES I AM Solution for dealing
    with control 57
    Task for right now 61

Chapter Four—Taking Steps Toward the Goal **63**
  Form a Supportive Committee 64
    Example of a how a supportive committee
    may *not* work 64
    Task for right now 65
  Create Your Vision 66
    Examples of Vision Statements 66
    Task for right now 67

Use Strong Communication Tools · 68
    Examples of methods of communication · · · · · · · · · · · · · 68
    Task for right now · 69
Segment the Project · 71
    Examples of Segmenting · 72
    Task for right now · .72

Chapter Five—Institutionalizing the Change · · · · · · · · · · · · · · · · · · · **75**
Relate to the Vision and Continue to Build · · · · · · · · · · · · · · · · · 76
    Examples of Relating to the Vision and
    Continuing to Build · 76
    Task for right now · 77
Integrate into the Organization's Culture · · · · · · · · · · · · · · · · · · · 78
    Examples of Integrating into the Organization's Culture · 78
    Task for right now · 79

Chapter Six—Change Examples: From Good to Awful · · · · · · · · · · · **81**
Successful Changes · 82
    American Airlines Maintenance Operations
    (a most amazing example) · 82
    Engineering Design Quality · 84
    Alan's Story · 87
Change So-So's · 89
    Electronics System Company · 89
    Medical Services Company · 91
Failures · 93
    AOL/Time-Warner · 93
    An ERM System · 94

Chapter Seven—Change Failed? Not Yours! · · · · · · · · · · · · · · · · · · · **97**
The Anxious Leader · 99
    Meet Laura, an Anxious Leader · · · · · · · · · · · · · · · · · · · 99
    Some Help for the Anxious Leader · · · · · · · · · · · · · · · · 101
The Confident Leader · 103
    Meet Anne, a Confident Leader · · · · · · · · · · · · · · · · · · 103
    Some Help for the Confident Leader · · · · · · · · · · · · · · 104

EXPANDED TABLE OF CONTENTS

The Hurried Leader · 107
    Meet Joleen, the Hurried Leader · · · · · · · · · · · · · · · · · 107
    Some Help for the Hurried Leader · · · · · · · · · · · · · · · · 108
The "Educated" Leader · 110
    Meet Art, the "Educated" Leader · · · · · · · · · · · · · · · · · 110
    Some Help for the Educated Leader · · · · · · · · · · · · · · · 111
The Mistrustful Leader · 113
    Meet Matt, the Mistrustful Leader · · · · · · · · · · · · · · · · 113
    Some Help for the Mistrustful Leader · · · · · · · · · · · · · · 114
The Uninformed Leader · 116
    Meet Jean and Jan, two types of Uninformed Leaders · · 116
    Some Help for the Uninformed Leader · · · · · · · · · · · · · 118
The Wrong-Change Leader · 120
    Meet Dante, the Wrong-Change Leader · · · · · · · · · · · · · 120
    Some Help for the Wrong-Change Leader · · · · · · · · · · · 121

Epilogue & Summary · **123**
The change that challenged me to lead… (cont.) · · · · · · · · · · 123
    Mel's request · 123
    Follow up meetings · 124
    Five months later · 125
The basic model revisited · 126
    Remember Your Situation · 127
    This book contains a lot · 127

List of Appendices · **129**
Appendix A—Expanded Table of Contents · · · · · · · · · · · · · 131
Appendix B—What Kind of Change Leader Are You? · · · · · · 135
    Interpret your scores · 137
Appendix C—Types of change and how they appear · · · · · · · · 139
Appendix D—Short history of change · · · · · · · · · · · · · · · · 141
Bibliography · **143**

Appendix B

WHAT KIND OF CHANGE LEADER ARE YOU?

This set of statements will help you identify your personal patterns when leading a change initiative. Respond based on your past behaviors. High numbers in some Leaders' categories will indicate where there is room for improvement.

Rate the statements below about your thoughts and feelings when introducing a change. Score on this scale: 5 strongly agree, 4 agree, 3 neutral, 2 disagree and 1 strongly disagree. Then total your score for each of the Leaders.

1. *Anxious Leaders*

___I worry that the change may not produce the desired benefits.

___I doubt my knowledge about the details of the change.

___I am worried about how I will be affected if the change fails.

___**Total**

2. *Confident Leaders*

___I feel solidly in control of the project and don't need help from anyone.

___I am sure that this will be an easy change based on my experiences.

___ I know how to employ the change process so I don't need help from my employees.

___ Total

3. *Hurried Leaders*

___ I believe that there may not be enough time to involve the employees in the planning.

___ I notice that something isn't working well but think I have gone too far to change.

___ I don't have time to explain to the employees how they will benefit from the change.

___ Total

4. *"Educated" Leaders*

___ I think I am well informed about the details of the desired change.

___ I believe I am using the appropriate change tools but don't get the expected results.

___ I might say "Here is what I think you should do. Are you okay with that?"

___ Total

5. *Mistrustful Leaders*

___ I believe that my employees are not interested in anything other than a paycheck.

___I am certain that my employees don't care about the change.

___I doubt there is value in the various tools that the change experts recommend.

___**Total**

6. *Uninformed Leaders*

___I don't understand why I don't achieve the results I want.

___I am surprised to learn that change often fails.

___I doubt that my employees are able to provide any useful help.

___**Total**

7. *Wrong Change Leaders*

___I make changes without clear goals

___I make changes before I understand the situation thoroughly

___I make changes because it seems like the right thing to do.

___**Total**

Interpret your scores

Total your points for each Leader type; the maximum is 15; the minimum is 3. Notice for which Leader types you score the highest. These are areas where you can develop your skills.

For those of you whose scores are uniformly low, that's great. I encourage you to use the book to do even better.

Appendix C

TYPES OF CHANGE AND HOW THEY APPEAR

Change surrounds us, but often goes unrecognized. The way we speak about activities may hide the inherent changes under consideration.

We face change when bringing on a new employee, or when we introduce a new product or process; change may come in the form of a merger with another company. In each of these cases, others in the organization will be affected. But when we don't explicitly state that we are pursuing a change, the fact of the change may be hidden. Ignoring the change can impede the activity's success. Its achievement depends on how others involved respond and work.

Each of these events has the potential to provide important benefits to the organization or cost it dearly! Which do you want?

Changes often come about by our choices—through our intentions. That is, someone has decided that the change is needed.

But changes can also be *forced* on us or may occur without us even being aware until we are well into the process.

Let's look at a few of these cases:

Sometimes we choose to make a change such as introducing an improved manufacturing process. We recognize that installing new equipment is a change. Similarly, adding a second shift creates a change. Moving a production facility offshore is also a change.

Sometimes change is thrust upon us when market conditions change rapidly; for example, when a market is deregulated (or newly regulated) and competition grows. Other examples could include the appearance of a new technology which could make our products obsolete, or the unexpected scarcity of a key component. Change is forced on us when a key service is interrupted. It happened in New York City many years ago when a major telephone switching center had a fire causing large areas of New York to lose phone service—in some cases, for weeks. [27] [28] And of course we must not forget 9/11! Or hurricane Sandy in 2012. In addition to the human loss, these events caused changes in power delivery, road closures, and the relocation of whole businesses.

Sometimes events drive change, but we do not recognize that change is occurring. Our company is growing, adding production facilities, staff, etc., and we think of these processes as "normal." And they are—but even normal events often involve change which may need to be managed.

In many of these cases, we may think that we have solid personal knowledge and that we have sought good advice as well. We are sure we can handle the situation ourselves. But we face risk in all of these cases if there are key issues we don't know about. Perhaps our employees have some important knowledge which could help improve the whole change process, but in our certainty, we fail to see these gaps in our knowledge. And that can lead directly to failure. We may even be introducing the *wrong* change!

Appendix D

SHORT HISTORY OF CHANGE

Change has been going on for a long time. As far back as 1776, Adam Smith described the idea of the division of labor in his book, *The Wealth of Nations* [29]. He pointed out that craftsmen (and in those days they were all men!) were being very inefficient when one person did all parts of a complex task. He observed that the production of a simple pin remarkably consisted of eighteen distinct steps such as cutting the wire, straightening the wire and so on. All of these tasks had been done by a single person. That person could, with effort, make as many as twenty pins in a day, and often as few as just one. Smith reported seeing a small "manufactory" where ten men were employed, each doing up to three of the tasks. This group of ten was producing about twelve pounds of pins in a day; at 4000 pins in a pound, that is about 48,000 pins!

Switching from a single person making all the parts of each pin to members of a team performing the individual steps resulted in over 250 times the output per person—*that* was a major change!

In the next century, in 1858 an underwater wire cable was installed from Ireland to Newfoundland which allowed people to send Morse Code across the Atlantic Ocean, providing for the first time the ability to communicate almost instantly between Europe and North America. This replaced the weeks of time previously required to send a message the same distance—that really changed things!

And what about telephone, movies, television, flight, not to mention computers and the Internet? They all resulted in major changes in society and in the businesses which were born from them.

Today we continually see changes or attempts at change in many areas: the environment, education, health, finance and more. These changes are often critical to the organization. Yet in many cases, the benefits are delayed or never occur.

I hope this book helps you be among the successful leaders who achieve the benefits you want and need.

BIBLIOGRAPHY

[1] W. Bennis, On Becoming a Leader, Philadelphia, PA: Basic Books; Fourth Edition, p. 42, 2009.

[2] P. Morley, "Research Findings on Program Failure and Success," 10 December 2008. [Online]. Available: https://www.maninthemirror.org/a-look-in-the-mirror/121-research-findings-on-program-failure-and-success. [Accessed 24 06 2012].

[3] #NumberOf.Net, "Number of MBA Graduates in the US per Year," 24 June 2010. [Online]. Available: http://www.numberof.net/number%C2%A0of%C2%A0mba%C2%A0graduates%C2%A0in-the-us-per%C2%A0year/. [Accessed 03 08 2012].

[4] Isaac Newton, Letter to Robert Hooke, February 5, 1675. [Online]. Available: The Quotation Page, http://www.quotationspage.com/quote/862.html [Accessed 24 06 2015].

[5] S. Keller and C. Aiken, "The Inconvenient Truth About Change Management," [Online]. Available: http://www.mckinsey.com/App_Media/Reports/Financial_Services/The_Inconvenient_Truth_About_Change_Management.pdf. [Accessed 19 07 2012].

[6] G. T. Doran, "There's a S.M.A.R.T. way to write management's goals and objectives.," Management Review, pp. 35-36, 1981.

[7] A. S. Tannenbaum, "Control in Organizations: Individual Adjustment and Organizational Performance," ADMINISTRATIVE SCIENCE QUARTERLY, pp. 236-257, 1962.

[8] J. P. Kotter, Leading Change, Cambridge, MA: Harvard Business Review Press, 1996.

BIBLIOGRAPHY

[9] K. Johnston, "What Is the Directional Function of Corporate Vision?," [Online]. Available: http://smallbusiness.chron.com/directional-function-corporate-vision-14595.html. [Accessed 20 07 2012].

[10] Amazon.com, "Amazon Vision Statement," 2014. [Online]. Available: http://phx.corporate-ir.net/phoenix.zhtml?c=97664&p=irol-faq#14296.

[11] IKEA, "IKEA Vision Statement," [Online]. Available: http://www.ikea.com/ms/en_IE/about_ikea/the_ikea_way/our_business_idea/index.html.

[12] Pepsico, "Pepsico Vision Statement," 2014. [Online]. Available: http://www.pepsico.com/Purpose/Our-Mission-and-Values.

[13] American Society for the Prevention of Cruelty to Animals, "ASPCA Vision Statement," 2014. [Online]. Available: http://www.aspca.org/about-us/aspca-polic-and-position-statements/vision.

[14] P. Schnitzler, Research Labs spending–Personal knowledge.

[15] S. Cline, "'Mission Accomplished' Bush's Infamous Iraq War Speech, 10 Years Later - Press Past (usnews.com)," U. S. News, 1 may 2013. [Online]. Available: http://www.usnews.com/news/blogs/press-past/2013/05/01/the-other-symbol-of-george-w-bushs-legacy. [Accessed 27 july 2013].

[16] W. Goodwyn, "American Airlines 'Insources' Maintenance Work," 7 December 2006. [Online]. Available: http://www.npr.org/templates/story/story.php?storyId=6594273.

[17] PRNewswire-FirstCall, "American Airlines Maintenance Services, Allegiant Air Enter Into Four-Year Contract," 18 December 2006. [Online]. Available: http://www.redorbit.com/news/business/771400/american_airlines_maintenance_services_allegiant_air_enter_into_fouryear_contract /.

[18] J. Stark, "A FEW WORDS ABOUT CONCURRENT ENGINEERING," 1998. [Online]. Available: http://www.johnstark.com/fwcce.html. [Accessed 1 7 2012].

[19] P. Schnitzler, Private communications from company manager, October 2009.

[20] P. Schnitzler,, Private communications from former professional employees of the company. [Interview]. August 2014.

[21] T. Johnson, "Internet leader and entertainment firm to join forces; new company worth $350B," 10 1 2000. [Online]. Available: http://money.cnn.com/2000/01/10/deals/aol_warner/. [Accessed 29 6 2012].

[22] Lehrer, Jim–PBS Newshour, "Bad Marriage? AOL Time Warner," 19 7 2002. [Online]. Available: http://www.pbs.org/newshour/bb/business/july-dec02/aoltime_7-19.html. [Accessed 29 9 2012].

[23] E. Barnett and A. Andrews, "AOL merger was 'the biggest mistake in corporate history', believes Time Warner chief Jeff Bewkes," 28 9 2010. [Online]. Available: http://www.telegraph.co.uk/finance/newsbysector/mediatechnologyandtelecoms/media/8031227/AOL-merger-was-the-biggest-mistake-in-corporate-history-believes-Time-Warner-chief-Jeff-Bewkes.html. [Accessed 29 6 2012].

[24] Larry Kramer – The Daily Beast, "Time Warner's decision last week to spin off AOL marks the end of a spectacularly failed merger. One that, Larry Kramer says, actually could have worked," 4 5 2009. [Online]. Available: http://www.thedailybeast.com/articles/2009/05/04/how-time-warner-blew-it.print.html. [Accessed 29 6 2012].

[25] P. Schnitzler, Private communications from company salesperson, 2012.

[26] Wikipedia, the free encyclopedia, "Submarine communications cable," 17 June 2012. [Online]. Available: http://en.wikipedia.org/w/index.php?title=Submarine_communications_cable&action=history. [Accessed 6 7 2012].

BIBLIOGRAPHY

[27] B. PORT, "Three Decades After An Infamous New York Telephone Co. Blaze, Cancer Ravages Heroes," 14 March 2004. [Online]. Available: http://articles.nydailynews.com/2004-03-14/news/18256332_1_fdny-telephone-fire-von-essen. [Accessed 06 08 2012].
[28] A. H. Wurtzel and T. Colin, "What Missing the Telephone Means," Journal of Communication, vol. 27, no. 2, p. 48–57, 2006.
[29] A. Smith, An Inquiry into the Nature and Causes of the Wealth of Nations, pp 8-9. [downloaded from:] http://political-economy.com/wealth-of-nations-adam-smith/ [Accessed 24-06-2015].

www.ingramcontent.com/pod-product-compliance
Lightning Source LLC
Chambersburg PA
CBHW051528170526
45165CB00002B/648